LIVIN' IN THE WORLD

Dave Hovey

© 2018 by Dave Hovey.
All rights reserved. No part of this book may be reproduced, stored in a retrieval system or transmitted in any form or by any means without the prior written permission of the publishers, except by a reviewer who may quote brief passages in a review to be printed in a newspaper, magazine or journal.

Third printing

All characters in this book are fictitious, and any resemblance to real persons, living or dead, is coincidental.

ISBN-13: 978-1-944583-16-3

Laurel Rose Publishing
www.laurelrosepublishing.com

Book and Jacket Style by Emma Hovey.
Photographs by Dave Hovey.

PROLOGUE

I reckon what my wife, Emma Ruth, says is pretty well right. She tells me this is not much of a book only a bunch of mischief better off forgotten. Maybe letting sleeping dogs lie would have been wiser. This growing up in good old Mississippi was such a fi ne experience, I just felt like all the poor deprived Yankee folks deserved to have a peep at what they missed out on.

Mississippi has almost caught up with the rest of the country now, especially in its two or three big cities. Our kids went to the bright lights and major paychecks like moths to the flame. They call me an old dinosaur for sort of refusing to change with them. My fiffty year old tractor still runs and I see no reason to trade it or Emma Ruth either one on some high dollar new model. Anyway I read someplace we are all products of our environment so a red neck I will always be. These stories are mostly about that very environment, a place like no other, gone but not forgotten by some.

CONTENTS

PROLOGUE 3

ACKNOWLEDGEMENTS 7

CHRISTMAS DELAYED 9
RISKY BUSINESS 12
INDELIBLE INK 13
THE ROAD TRIP 15
MR. WHISKERS 19
BROWN BAG LUNCH 22
FLYING TOAD 25
DEVILS WALKING STICKS 27
HORSESHOES "1944" 30
THE DAM 32
"SPEND THE NIGHT" 38
YELLOW FEVER 43
DOG HOME YET 50
"YOU DID WHAT?" 57
FAMILY FUN "1946" 60
TURTLE SOUP 63
THE FLOAT TRIP 67
THE BROWNS 70
LESTER'S SECRET 74
HAPPY DAYS 77
THE NEW TRACTOR 81
CAMP PUSHMATAHA 84
TOO MANY MELONS 91
OKLAHOMA VISITOR 94
REVENGE 97
THE PASSION PIT 99

COFFEEVILLE SATURDAY NIGHT	103
OLD ONE ELEVEN	106
THE COOL RIDE	109
THE WATER TANK	111
AUTOMOBILE DOCTORS	113
"SCAREDY CAT"	115
HOWARD'S RATTLESNAKE	117
THE FLAT TIRE	119
CALLING ALL FISH	121
OPENING DAY	124
PERSIMMON BEER	126
THE BIRD HOUND	128
DAIRY DELIGHT	131
AMBULANCE CHASERS	134
MIXED COMPANY	138
KOOL KOMFORT	141
NEW BOOTS	143
ASSASSINATION	146
THE ROYAL GORGE	150
"SUPER BOWL, MAYBE"	157
OUCH" THAT HURT	162
LONG PIG	165
SPOOKY AIRCRAFT TALES	169
FOURTH OF JULY	171
STREAKERS '1970'	175
JUNGLE DENTIST	177
MARTIAL DUTY	179
YOU REAP WHAT YOU SOW	183
WORKS CITED	190
EPILOGUE	191
BIO	193

ACKNOWLEDGEMENTS

For my brother, Jon, who knows which episodes had to be left out.

CHRISTMAS DELAYED

Tom was headed home in his wagon. Bob and Kate moved right along without being spoken to. They had stood patiently on Front Street at the wooden sidewalks while Tom used up part of his furnish arrangements. He had to be very careful in selecting the few oranges, apples and peppermint candy. It was still a long cold time until anything could be produced to settle the store accounts, a few eggs now and then and the sale of four piglets would help offset some bills but any cash money had to go toward taxes, school books or other necessary things.

All that aside, tomorrow was Christmas, two little girls and two little boys would be up at dawn to check the four stockings hanging from the fireplace mantle.

It was nearly dark by the time Tom rounded the last bend in the red sand road several miles from town. He had been studying hard on how to separate the Christmas fruit and candy from the other meager purchases. These needed to stay hidden until he could slip back out later and bring them in to fill the four stockings.

The boys ran to meet the wagon and unhitched for Tom when he pulled into the drive-thru wagon shed. The girls carried the sacks of salt, coffee and expensive sugar up to the house. Everybody was on their best behavior anticipating certain rewards in the morning.

The nice clean sage grass patch Tom had passed as he rounded that last bend seemed ideal. He had stopped the team, picked up the cardboard box of fruit and candy and hid it carefully across from the spring branch in the tall dry grass. The tow-sack used as a pad on the wooden wagon seat made a good cover over the box and unless you checked very close it was well hidden.

Nancy looked a question at him when he came into the lamp glow of the kitchen. He winked and smiled his answer and she smiled back reassured.

The kitchen table contained two big bowls of popcorn, one green and one pink. It was supposed to be red but the Watkins food color always just made it pink. The fresh cut cedar tree in the fireplace room corner already had several strands draped around it. The girls complained however, they said two strands had been removed earlier and one brother's mouth was green while the other's was extra red.

Nancy found each girl a needle and spool of white thread and they contentedly sewed more popcorn strands for replacements.

Granny had already carried the warm brick wrapped in a feed sack to put under the foot of her quilt and retired to her room.

The many trips to the windows to peep out into the moonlit sand yard finally slowed down and stopped.
Four small eyes in two beds were closed in sleep at last. Both fireplaces had burned down to coals against the bigger back log. Tom went to the kitchen, got his jacket and hat off the hooks by the door. Nancy quietly rocked by the fire and smiled again as he eased out into the night.

Tom trotted fast down the drive in the crisp frosty air. He had not bothered with a lantern since it was so bright and the box would be easy to find.

Something was wrong, the box lay on its side, and it was completely empty. Tom got down on hands and knees and searched hard in the sage grass. The grass was torn up and he smelled a hog smell. The rail fence pen was just a short distance away across the spring branch. Tom ran fast to see if the old sow and piglets were still there. The fence was knocked down but the old sow lay under the shed contentedly nursing the piglets.

Tom ran all the way back to tell Nancy in a panic. Whatever were they to do, nearly midnight on Christmas Eve and no presents to fill the stockings? Tears were in his eyes as he quietly told what had happened. Nancy made him sit down and fixed some coffee.

There just was not much to be done about it at this time of night. A bowl of popcorn remained on the table and she could fix more. They both worked until almost dawn fixing sorghum molasses popcorn balls to wrap in wax paper and put in the stockings. Tom said he would just have to fess up to what happened and try to make it up to the four children when the store opened Monday.

Mr. Cohea was very understanding. He chuckled and put two extra oranges into the new box. It had snowed pretty good Christmas day so a fine time was had with lots of company and good things to eat, including snow ice cream.

The popcorn ball stockings now were a topic that caused everyone to laugh. Oranges and candy for a Monday lunch had also made a never to be forgotten treat. Christmas "1909" is still remembered each year at a certain farm house out on Turkey Creek.

RISKY BUSINESS

My first risqué situation, that I can remember, happened in the second grade. Our school that year consisted of fifteen students. The blackboard was divided up into the maximum six sections, third grade was blank. No third graders this time. Next year unless new arrivals appeared there would be no fourth grade.

Two older girls had been jumping rope. When I closed the outhouse door they slipped up and eased it open enough to peep inside.

When I came out they were giggling so hard tears ran down their cheeks. I asked what was so funny. The red headed one "Eunice" said "spell oil cup and leave out the L". That broke them up again into gales of merriment.

I was not to sure how to spell "oil cup" anyway and sort of missed the punch line. Not being one to waste a good joke even if I didn't get it, I told it to my pretty little classmate Joan. She quickly spelled it out very loud and when I dutifully "hee-hawed" she blushed and ran inside to tell it to Mrs. Sundberg, our heavy set, no nonsense, Swedish school teacher.

The short piece of rubber hose smarted enough to bring tears to anybody's eyes. It was a long, long time before I ever tried to tell another joke. In fact it was a year or two later before I finally figured that one out.

INDELIBLE INK

Country schools were pretty much alike before the WWII. Our school was one room with a big blackboard across the back behind the teacher's desk.

Our desks were all fastened to a set of wooden runners, on down to the foot of each row. Every row was a different grade, one through six. The blackboard was also divided up into six sections, but it was my desk that caused a problem.

Nobody had ever heard of a ball point pen yet. We each received a pencil, a ruler, a big Red Chief notebook and a wood pen with a sharp silver point. The school provided these items along with a bottle of ink that fit in a hole in the front of the desk.

I really liked Norma Johnson who sat directly in front of me in third grade. She undoubtedly was the prettiest girl in Evergreen school. Almost all the girls wore pigtails with rubber bands or little cloth bows. Some wore two, others like Norma just one beautifully plaited golden braid halfway down her back.

It flopped tantalizingly close on my desk, next to the ink well. To make a long story short, my pen and ink well were permanently confiscated. That piece of rubber hose got all the dust out of my back overall pockets. Norma's mama called my mama and I got dusted again that night at home. It took awhile for Norma's pigtail to reach my desk again but the ink bottle was gone now anyway. The chap that invented ball point pens saved lots of purple fingers, desk stains and quite a few pigtails. I just wished he had his idea a little sooner.

THE ROAD TRIP

Dec. 7th 1941,

Roosevelt was right; he had just said it was a day that would live in infamy. The grownups were all clustered around the battery powered Philco radio in the kitchen. We had a large houseful of company, Uncles, Aunts and a sack full of cousins of all ages. Pa told us to hush and find something to do outside. We whined and said it was too cold. He was trying to listen to the radio along with the two Uncles. He said go out to the road then and bring back the mail.

Our farm had a long dirt lane. The mailman would not drive the quarter mile up to the house so our box was placed on the main road.

Toody was with us as usual. Ma seemed to expect him being around all the time. Pa never seemed to mind one way or the other. My little brother was playing some game in the fireplace room with our girl cousins and the smaller kids. He was only seven; Toody and me were nine and didn't think of ourselves as little kids anymore.

It really was cold out; the wind from the North even had a touch of sleet.

Pa's "36" Model Ford car was parked under the big cottonwood tree next to the drive. He would put it under the shed later, but both our Uncle's cars had parked around behind to get closer to the kitchen door with the food.

Toody and I had been taught to drive Pa's John Deere tractor. We only had to sit on it and steer. Pa would set the throttle and we could pull or push the hand clutch to go or stop. It went real slow and he had us drive while they pulled corn or some other chores close by. Cars at that time didn't need a key. You flipped a little silver switch on the steering column to shut the thing off or on.

I looked sideways at Toody when he said, "as cold as it is we better take the car". I was a bit surprised but smiled and agreed.

Getting behind the wheel, I pulled out the choke knob and flipped the switch on just as I had closely watched Pa do so many times. He would then reach over and shake the tall gearshift stick back and forth to make certain it was out of gear. Toody watched me close to be sure I did it correctly; he also had observed Pa many times in the past.

I pushed the little round silver button on the dashboard and it started right up. With the wind and the kids both howling, the women yakking loud over the sound of the radio, nobody heard the Ford motor running.

The first problem arose when I scrunched way down to mash the clutch and pull the tall shift into gear. I was now flying blind, no longer able to see over the dash. Toody was a quick study; he noticed this situation right away and grabbed the steering wheel as my foot released the clutch. The thing immediately went dead. Toody said you forgot to push on the gas pedal.

I got set and went back through the whole routine only this time using both feet, one on the gas as well, Toody had the steering covered. Luckily, we were more or less headed out the driveway. The Ford spun its wheels and shot forward. When I rose up it just continued to poke along down the drive at an idle. Concerned with staying in the tracks neither of us thought about more speed. Toody let me take over the steering and soon we came to the main road.

I pulled the wheel and made the turn out all right, but forgot to quickly spin it back the other way. The Ford continued in a circle right off into the ditch and choked to a stop.

We both knew that reverse was where you pushed the gear lever straight toward the dash. Back through the starting routine again and it cranked up. When I took my foot off the clutch this time instead of flying backward, the tires just spun, while the motor roared. We were stuck. I flipped the little switch down and we climbed out for a look. The front wheels were almost out of sight in the weeds.

Taking the car for the mail suddenly seemed like a bad idea. Toody said he really needed to be heading on home. He was sort of backing that way already. I walked over and shut the door, then opened the mailbox for the paper and stuff, and started slowly for the house.

I handed Pa the mail and must have looked kind of troubled. He asked me if anything was the matter and glanced around for Toody. For some reason he always watched us closer when Toody was there.

I said, "Well, it looks like I might need a little help with the Ford". Pa's chair fell over as he jumped up and popped over to the window. When he turned back, his face was already getting red. Mine was turning very white. "What do you mean, help with the Ford?" he shouted. "Where is it?"When I told him we got stuck as we turned around on the way to get the mail, he looked even worse. Both Uncles were laughing so hard they nearly fell out of their chairs. Ma had her hand over her mouth. My girl cousins were merrily giggling with anticipation, my brother's eyes were as round as saucers.

Uncle Bud jumped up and grabbed Pa by the arm. Tears were coming out of his eyes. He said, "come on lets go get it back." I always had a fine opinion of him from that day on. All three of them got in Uncle Bud's pickup and in a short time; Pa pulled the Ford into its shed.

He told me he would tan my hide if I ever messed with the car again. I could tell though that he was trying hard not to smile and some tears were still on his eyes also.

MR. WHISKERS

Pa was already gone to town in his old Ford pickup; Ma was busy in the kitchen at the back of the house. My little brother Jon and me were warming up in front of the fireplace in the big bedroom, where Pa and Ma slept.

Doves had called that very morning. We heard them good with the windows all opened for the first time since last fall.

Boss and Beanie our two Red Bone hounds suddenly set in to making a racket. They bayed and barked, somebody was saying "Here now", in a deep voice. Steps sounded on the back porch followed by a loud tapping on the porch post.

We jumped up and sailed out to the kitchen to find Ma talking to an old chap in a shabby tore up Mackinaw coat. Ma had him setting at the oilcloth table a few minutes later with a mug of coffee in his dirty hand. She fixed a plate of fried eggs and salt meat along with our leftover breakfast biscuits. We stood by the wood stove big eyed as the little old man ate everything in sight.

Ma shooed us out into the yard to get some corn shelled with the Blackhawk sheller on the wood box. We fed the chickens, tried to nail the big old red rooster with a few cobs and gathered some eggs.

Coming back into the house, arms full of short stove wood, we were eager to find out more about our strange visitor. Boss and Beanie had finished their wooden trough of mush and grease. They dozed in the back porch sun. The interesting visitor was gone. Ma said she just felt sorry for him. He had walked up from the railroad about a half mile over across the creek bottom.

It was the following March a year later almost to the day, another bright spring morning. Jon and me were in the barn loft tossing down the last of the hay to some calves Pa was weaning. Boss and Beanie bayed and barked but quickly hushed. We heard that deep "Here now" and a loud tapping on the porch post.

He wore the same tattered plaid Mackinaw coat and patched overalls. Ma already had him a mug of coffee when we popped in the back door. Ma was holding up a great big wooden handled butcher knife. It was brand new, shiny with copper rivets in the handle, and twice as big as any of our other knives

Mr. Whiskers asked us our names squinting with a sort of toothless smile. He held out his dirty hand for us to shake. We weren't about to get that close to him. Ma just laughed as she set him out a big breakfast again.

He took a lot longer to eat this time. Ma and him sat and chatted like old friends. We stood behind the water box on the stove and listened. Ma ran us out to do chores. Later Mr. Whiskers was sort of leaning on a cedar walking stick heading toward the foot log over the creek on his way back to the railroad. The trains would slow and stop for waiting cars of pulpwood just outside of town.

When Pa came home, Ma showed him the big new knife. He admired it saying it was a fine piece of work.

Ma said Mr. Whiskers told her he made them with hand files from broken pieces of band saw blades.

For the next three years on very nearly the same day in March, Ma got a new knife. They were not alike; each was a different size and shape, smaller than the first.

Pa had left instructions to Ma along with a five-dollar bill. Mr. Whiskers never said thanks or anything, but he stuck the money in a little fold up snap purse after he ate his breakfast. We shook hands and even let him pat our heads and talk to us now.

Five visits was it, we never saw him again. I do not think Ma ever learned his whole name or much else about him. He never came back to see us.

There were many men riding the freight cars just before the big war. They came south in the fall and rode north in the spring. The war put everybody back to work in a hurry and pretty well ended the hobo life style.

Now it is back with us again except we call them "homeless." If you visit any big city, you will see many down and out folks pushing shopping carts, sleeping in alleys and doorways and asking for handouts on the street. I hope there is a better way to solve the problem this time than another big world war. Seems to be true that history always repeats itself.

BROWN BAG LUNCH

On many warm fall days, we chose the field route to school, using the shortcut, which was actually longer.

While looking for a crows nest we noticed a baby squirrel going into a hole. After climbing the tree Toody's hand popped out with a big brown bat hanging off his finger. He let his other hand go to pull on the bat and fell to the ground on his back in the grass.

My first thought naturally was to save that bat. Even with both wings pinched together, he would not turn Toody's finger loose.

Toody could talk again some now, I can't repeat what he said but he sure wanted that bat off his finger. I shouted for my little brother Jon to spill out my lunch sack into his, and then slipped the bag over the bat. Maybe the dark would make him turn loose. It worked great; Jon squeezed the bag shut over the bat.

Later our impromptu "Show and Tell" was a fine success. Toody liked asking girls to peek at what was in the bag. It sent them off screeching. The boys were just curious. Most had never seen a bat up close and personal.

The bell rang so everyone went in to their desk. Toody set the bat bag on the cloakroom shelf against the wall over the stove wood.

The bat was forgotten in the lunchtime excitement and games. In fact, he was still there in his bag when Ms. Sundberg came in the next morning. As usual, she did a sweep and clean before we all arrived. When we got there a few minutes later, it was just in time to witness an extraordinary sight.

A loud piercing scream split the air as both double doors flew wide open. Ms. Sundberg was a lot more than slightly heavyset, but she could easily have sprinted past any one of us just then. She whoa-ed up, turning big eyed, both hands on top of the gate looking back at the schoolroom. Thinking someone forgot their lunch or part of it, she had taken the bag down off the shelf, reaching inside for the expected sandwich wrapped in wax paper or maybe an apple or sweet potato. Instead, something furry and alive began crawling up her wrist. We witnessed the results of this but only quick-witted Toody remembered and guessed what set things in motion.

Toody calmly marched into the one room school. He found the straw broom and spotted Mr. Bat in a corner of the ceiling. A whack and miss or two and Mr. Bat sailed out the door. Don't believe that stuff about how they only can see in the dark.

Toody stood the broom against the wall and triumphantly headed out toward the gate.

He said, "That old bat is gone now teacher, you can come back in. Ms. Sundberg wiped her eyes, sniffed and crushed Toody's head in a fine big hug. She said "Thank you Toody, I don't know how I would get along without you." I guess they both forgot about the many times Toody had been on the other end of the peach switch.

Later on that morning, I saw Ms. Sundberg watching Toody with her normal scowl. It probably just dawned on her how that bag happened to be on that shelf and who most likely put it there.

FLYING TOAD

"Pa" showed us how to take a big red bandana kerchief, which we had plenty of, and make a parachute. Four pieces of white store string tied to each corner and all tied together into a good sized nut off a bolt had it ready. You folded it back and forth over the strings with the nut underneath. An underhand toss worked best, it would fly up into the air and float down on the breeze.

Not long after "Pa" left we moved to the barn hay loft door to gain more height. When Toody went to retrieve his parachute a big hop toad was sitting right by it. The next step was inevitable; the toad replaced the nut for weight and soon became airborne. He made a number of successful jumps none the worse for wear.

"Pa" used carbide powder in his coon hunting light. The stuff came in a quart metal can and looked like gray pea gravel. When water dripped onto a small amount it put off acetylene gas which made the light. "Pa" explained to us how you put a spoonful into the bottom of an empty paint can with a press on lid. You punched a nail hole on the side of the can at the bottom. A simple two-step process made it work. One, remove the lid, spit on the carbide and press the lid back on firmly. Two, keep your head out of the way and touch a lighted match to the hole near the base. "Ka-wham", the lid would fly high into the air. It was better than fireworks but you had to be careful not to put in too much carbide.

The toad was already somewhat dazed so he sat quietly on the folded bandana placed on top of the paint can lid. Toody touched off the match; he had put in an extra spoonful for the increased weight. "Ka-wham", that toad went up nearly out of sight. The chute opened nicely as Mr. Toad descended slowly around in front of the house.

Bro. McGregor and his wife had nearly come to a stop in front of the gate when the toad landed on their car's hood. They both sat still for a few minutes looking at it. The hood was sort of hot so the toad hopped off dragging his parachute. Mr. Toad slid off the fender and hit the ground on the driver's side. Bro McGregor picked up the red bandana with the toad hanging and wiggling and looked up at the sky. His wife was looking up as well. Ma met them at the gate, we watched from around the corner of the house. She didn't know how it all came about but she knew good and well who caused the toad to arrive by parachute.

We came out when called to make our explanation and confession. That was the hardest I ever saw that preacher laugh. Always after that whenever we smiled at him at church he would just bust out with a big he-haw. Pa got tickled about it too, but Ma never did think it was all that amusing.

DEVILS WALKING STICKS

Late one summer, before the 1950's start of DDT poison, there were still all kinds of bugs and birds.

The truck garden beside the house was patrolled daily by Grandma and Ma. They would pull the big green tobacco worms off the tomatoes and eggplants. Garrett's powdered snuff would be sprinkled on peppers, cabbage, potatoes and cauliflowers. Wood ashes spread around the base of fruit trees and plants. Epsom salts under melons, tomatoes and squash. Many other tried and proven remedies including Marigold's growing among the peas and corn really did help a lot.

We, of course, were supposed to assist in these garden duties. Our time after school and during vacation was already partly used up with regular chores, bringing water from the spring on wash days, feeding chickens, hogs, cows and so forth. Milking was done early each morning before walking to school. It seemed like there was never a time when somebody didn't want something done.

Not until years later did we realize how Pa and sometimes Ma cleverly made certain we had a little time of our own.

Grandma had the three of us in the garden one hot August Saturday, pulling weeds and picking butterbeans all at the same time. Toody could have gone back home but being always at our place the big folks expected him to help out as well.

Pa walked up to the garden fence and said, "You boys come with me." A big sweet gum had toppled into the edge of the field during a storm a few nights ago. Pa wanted us to carry off the brush he had chopped free. The main trunk had been dragged off with the John Deere tractor to be cut into firewood later on.

When we walked into the shade behind the barn, he said, "wait here a minute." He came out with a large mason jar and two wooden thread spools. The jar contained two big praying mantis bugs each four or five inches long. They were green and brown with long legs and arms like people.

Taking one out of the jar he held it by its two wings. The thing would twist its head and try to bite. They could bite pretty hard. We had watched them in the weeds; they would hold another bug in their arms and gobble it up. He had trimmed their wings with his pocket knife. All they could do now was run or walk.

Each empty wooden spool, from Ma's sewing machine, had a smooth twig stuck through it. Both ends had a short piece of string tied to them. The dirt behind the barn was packed smooth. Pa said, "Hold his wings while I hook up his harness." I carefully pinched old Mr. Mantis out of his fingers as he tied both strings around its trailing back end. Toody helped get the next one fixed.

Two lines were now scratched in the dirt about ten feet apart. The race was ready to begin.

Pa held one in position with the little wagon behind it. I held the other as instructed beside it not quite touching the ground.

On the command "Go" both bugs hit the dirt racing toward freedom. Those things really could move out. Frantically flapping the stubs of their wings they dashed straight forward pulling the spools and looking like small harness racers, mine won.

Pa left to go move brush, he had never intended for us to help him, just used that excuse to sneak us away from the garden.

We already were planning to find another Devils Walking Stick for Jon so it would be a three way race. Also it would be good to have some replacements when these bugs wore out.

Nowadays my grandchildren sit on a couch in air conditioned comfort, mashing buttons on a little electronic device, watching strange Mantis like creatures race each other across the TV screen. Instead of being tanned, lean and energetic they are pale, chubby and lethargic.

Makes me wonder what folks will look like two or three generations from now.

HORSESHOES "1944"

In the warm times of the year we only wore shoes on Sunday or special occasions. We had to put on our heavy ankle top Brogans for Church and Sunday School.

As soon as Church let out, while the big folks stood around outside catching up on the latest gossip, my brother and me would race down the dirt road looking for beer cans in the borrow ditches. Soda's only came in bottles then. When we found a can we would stomp on the middle until it wrapped tight around our Brogans.

We soon had a fine pair of horseshoes and would trot up and down the road with a clickety, clatter, and clack. Sometimes our horseshoes would remain on our Brogans under the bed until the following Sunday. We were then forced to remove them to start the cycle all over again.

Getting dressed on a weekday morning was a simple chore. You just tossed back a quilt, jumped out of your corn shuck mattress, grabbed a pair of torn, dusty, overalls off the bare wood floor, hooked up one gallus clip and flew out to the kitchen. Underwear like Brogans was thankfully reserved for special occasions. (I still can't stand the stuff). I well remember on hot fall days, going to school with no shirt or shoes and nobody thought a thing about it. Somehow I made it through the sixth grade. My brother went on to graduate from the town high school. He rode a bus our neighbor put together out of an old truck. They tried to convince me to go also. Even though the peach limb smarted, the sixth was my last full year. I still get a warm happy feeling whenever I recall walking out that town school door and setting out across the fields and woods for home. It was one of the best days of my life and I would do the same thing again without hesitation. Emma Ruth says that's a terrible example to set and I guess she is right for this day and time. Things were different back then. Working hard with your hands or back was respected and rewarded. I was driving a Studebaker car while others my age had to ask for quarters to go to the picture show. There is more than one kind of education, as long as you get taught the rules in the Good Book and try to stay within its bounds. You should be able to choose your own path. Most of this country's best politicians and leaders were the ones with more horse sense than book sense. We need another one up there now.

Train up a child in the way he should go and when he is old he will not depart from it. Proverbs 22: 6.

THE DAM

Pa made an acquaintance with Mr. Bond and he invited us out to their big fine house in the country. Mr. Jack Bond made his living as an artist. He painted in watercolor and was very much in demand. People had him paint pictures of their homes or farms, even portraits.

We arrived on a hot July morning in our 1936 Blue Ford Sedan. Pa had the windshield cranked open to let in the breeze. The forty-mile trip had taken a couple of hours on dusty roads.

The first thing me and my little brother noticed when we got out on the circle drive was a brand new black Nash car. While the grownups exchanged pleasantries, we walked all around that Nash. The Bonds polite little boy Billy followed us and asked if we would like to see inside of it. He was eight, same age as my brother. I was ten and could drive our Ford and the tractor. Billy opened the door and said they call this the car you step down into. Most cars of the time had running boards, this one you really did step over and down into.

Billy's mom called and said for us to wash up for lunch. We followed Billy up the brick steps, past the big white columns and up a wide staircase to his bathroom on the second floor. The house was carpeted all over with mirrors and fancy furniture everywhere. We had never been in a place like this before.

We washed in the sink and left the snow-white towels sort of gray in places. Following Billy to the glass-enclosed sunroom, we found a small table set just for kids.

The grownups were in the dining room at a great big old table. A lady with a strange accent came in and out of a swinging door with dishes and trays of stuff for the big folks. We had sandwiches and tomato soup. It was great but somebody had cut all the crust off the bread and that was the part I liked best. The lady brought us big pieces of lemon pie with fluffy stuff on top for desert.

Billy's Pa, Mr. Jack called to Billy through the open door. He said, "Show the boys around outside when you finish your lunch. We jumped up and headed out a back door in the sunroom.

Billy showed us their garage containing a pickup truck and another car. It was an older model Hudson. He had a swing set just like the kind they had in the park in town. We told him ours was a rubber tire on a rope.

Coming in to their farm, we had crossed a bridge over a nice creek. It ran along one side of their place and there was a big concrete structure not far away on the skyline. I asked Billy what that building was. Billy said, "Oh, that's not a building it's a cement dam on the creek and just above it is a big lake.

My little brother Jon looked at me and grinned. We could often read each other's thoughts. It was very hot even for a July afternoon. I told Billy a creek runs past one side of our farm too and we swim in it to cool off lots of times.

Billy said he did not know how to swim and had never been in his creek. Jon was already starting off across the wheat stubble; the field had been cut a few days before. Billy hung back; he said my Mother told me not to go down to the creek.

I hollered back and told him, "Ok, we are going to cool off, stay here if you want too".

We reached the creek bank and started to look for a good swimming hole. Billy came puffing up all red faced and sweaty. He was not a fat kid, but was puny looking with pale skin and skinny arms and legs. Me and Jon worked and played outside all the time, mostly without shirt or shoes. Our feet could walk on hot coals, and the sun had turned us a very dark brown.

There was a loud racket coming from up the creek toward the cement structure. Jon lead the way at a trot, "Wow", water rolled and boiled into a big basin just below the dam. It whirled and swirled over some big rocks out in the middle.

Jon and me hung our clothes on a fence that came down the side of the dam. We eased out into the foam past waist deep and paddled out to the biggest rock. This was neat, the most exciting place we had ever seen to swim in. I slipped off the rock and stood up. The water came only up to my neck. The bottom was gravel and sand. My toes hit a good-sized stone so I stepped up on it.

The stone started to move with me standing on it. Jon was sitting on the big rock. Billy sat on the bank watching. I told Jon, "Get over here, dive down, and see why this rock is moving under my feet". He dove in and went to check it out. I had suspicioned it, and Jon confirmed it, when he popped up laughing. He said you are standing on a snapping turtle. The water was clear enough to see a little bit. The natural thing to do next was to try and catch that turtle. I knew if I stepped off, he would quickly swim away. I told Jon, "Go back down and grab him, but be sure to come from behind or he will latch on to your finger". When I felt Jon pull the turtle, I dove down to help. Jon had his tail in one hand and one hind foot. I grabbed his shell far enough back to keep from getting snapped and lifted him up over my head, scrambling quickly out onto the bank flipping Mr. Turtle on his back. Jon poked a short stick into his mouth, knowing he would not let it go. We had caught many turtles in our own creek. Ma cooked them if we dressed them. Jon pulled on the stick while I carved Mr. Turtles head off with my pocketknife. He was not going anyplace now, flopping on his back with feet in the air.

Jon was busy climbing up a concrete support ramp using the fence to hold onto. He said he wanted to look at the lake. I climbed behind him and was surprised to see Billy managing to come up also. Of course, Billy still had on his short pants. We all had left our shirts and tennis shoes at the swing set, our overalls hung on the fence. The lake was big, blue, and very deep right in front of the spillway. I told Jon I was going to dive off the top into the water and swim over to the grassy shore to come out. He said "no way, that water looks too deep".

The water sort of pulled at me and I swam hard to come back to the surface. It was not far to the shore where the shallow grassy bank met the wall of the dam.

We tossed a few rocks and went back to get our turtle and put on our clothes. The entire adventure was interesting but not much more eventful than other things we had done.

Not so with Billy, he was amazed, thrilled and just bubbling with enthusiasm. This had been one of the most adventuresome days of his life.

Jon perked up his ears and we set off across the wheat stubble field. Car horns were sounding loudly in the distance. It crossed my mind that we might be heading toward a less than friendly reception. The stubble scratched our toes some but not enough to really hurt.

Billy was lagging way behind, he also was crying and walking in a sort of skip and hop fashion. Pa and Mr. Jack met us part way. Pa looked at the big snapper with no head and said; "Well I guess you found the creek all right".

Mr. Jack frowned and moved fast toward Billy. He put Billy on his back and all of us came up onto the big front porch.

The women had gotten up out of their chairs and Billy's Mom was down on her knees in front of his chair. His feet were pretty bloody from the stubble and he had turned a bright shade of red all over.

The lady that talked funny came out with a dishpan of water and towels and stuff. Billy howled and yowled when they cleaned up his feet.

Mr. Jack said, "Where did you catch that old snapper?" Jon told him I was standing on it in the fast water below the dam. Mr. Jack turned sort of pale. He said, "Couldn't we read those no swimming signs all around that fence". I said no, the only one I noticed was when I dove off the top of the spillway. Mr. Jack looked at Pa in a funny way. He said the reason the sign was there is because of the suction created from the current in front of the dam. The water went down to a huge pipe with a grate over it. I could have easily been sucked down into that outlet.

Ma looked mad as a wet hen. She fussed over Billy while his Ma rubbed some kind of slippery oil over him. Pa was telling Mr. Jack he was sorry we got into so much mischief.

Billy perked up as we got ready to leave. He couldn't walk but he sat up in his chair and said please come back to play again. I never had that much fun before in my whole life.

Mr. Jack started to laugh and soon Pa was laughing too. Mr. Jack slapped Pa on the back and said, "Well no real harm done." Pa said next time for them to come and visit us. Billy's Ma smiled a crocodile smile and said yes very soon.

They never did show up for some reason. In fact, we never even saw Billy again but I know he always remembered our visit.

"SPEND THE NIGHT"

About once every couple of months, Ma would load up some canned jars of peaches, pickles, fresh greens and maybe ham or fried chicken. Uncle Lonzo and Aunt Lucille lived on a farm over in the next county. They had one boy named Billy and one girl named Dody (for Delores). She was twelve years old, Billy was eight same as my brother. I was ten that summer.

Their farm was smaller but bordered a much larger creek and had more bottom ground. Often they came to our place to visit the same way on a Saturday morning. We would attend each other's church after spending the night and return home on Sunday evening late.

Dody was the only girl cousin we really liked. She was tanned brown and skinny like us. The ones that lived near town, twin girls eleven years old never came to visit. Their Pa was a Methodist preacher and his heavyset wife didn't care for Ma for some reason. We only saw them at family reunions. Our other kinfolks just lived too far away since very few roads were paved in those days.

Lonzo and Pa had settled into the cane bottom rockers on the front porch. Ma and Lucille were cleaning up from lunch. It was awful hot, ninety-five in the shade.

The four of us kids were all sort of sweaty and dizzy from winding up one another in the rope tire swing. It hung from a big Chestnut oak limb in the sand yard.

When you finished your spin, you had to walk a straight line marked in the sand without falling over. Dody was the only one who could do it.

Billy brushed the sand from his face and hands; he had fallen over as soon as we got him out of the tire. He still looked a little green. He said, "Let's head down to the creek and cool off".

Some older neighbor boys liked to swim at this same deep hole in the creek on Lonzo's place. The red clay banks on Lonzo's side were tall. The other side was open pasture. They had fixed a rope swing from a big cottonwood tree. You could fly way out over the middle to turn loose and drop in. We had the place all to ourselves this day.

Dody had on her usual sleeveless flower print, feed sack dress. We wore overalls but no shirts. We never wore shoes except to Church or school and often not to school. None of us wanted anything to do with underwear.

Everybody peeled off and sailed down the bank after hanging their clothes on bushes to keep the ticks, redbugs and ants out of them.

It was such an exciting event and the cool creek so welcome, the fact that Dody jumped in too went completely unnoticed.

Billy said he could swing far enough out to drop in headfirst. All of us scrambled up the bank trying to be first on the rope. Dody beat us to it as usual.

She was pumping hard on that swing to go higher when my brother and I looked at each other. Billy seemed to find the situation quite normal. We had both realized it around the same time, I guess. My little brother sort of whispered in Billy's ear, "What happened to Dody?" Billy looked puzzled, he said, "I don't know, nothing I reckon".

Jon said, "I mean how come she has them parts missing?" He was only eight. I laughed and Billy frowned. He told Jon, "She ain't never been hurt, she's just a girl, and all girls are that away." That ended the discussion.

Dody had marvelously turned a flip off the swing. None of us could hope to compete on her level; we cheered and clapped our hands.

Everybody got dressed after drying off a bit in the sun. Dody said, "Let's go feed the ducks!" Billy said, "You better not do that again Dody, Ma told you she would wear you out next time."

Dody smiled her wicked, freckled faced smile and tore out for the tool shed in back of the house. Her blond pigtail flew straight on the breeze. We were fast but not that fast.

She came slipping out of the shed with a piece of trotline string wound around her hand. Billy said, "Uh, Oh; she better watch it." We followed her to the back of the smoke house. She was in there quite awhile, using the big knife to slit holes in five bite-sized pieces of raw fatback. Each greasy little piece was tied into the string about three feet apart.

The old black and white ducks had red combs like a rooster, only these hung over their beaks, like a turkey's goozle.

Dody tossed down the first piece tied on the string. A duck immediately swallowed it, the string hanging out of his beak. Dody gave him some slack. In just seconds, the fat back popped out behind the duck. It wouldn't stay on their stomachs so they passed it right on through.

Dody grabbed it up and dropped it in front of a smaller duck. Same thing happened. She now gave the first duck the next piece on the string. He squirted it out right in front of the small duck.

Soon five ducks were on the string, beak to tail. Dody tied the ends together. We all sat down to watch. The ducks kept trying to gobble up the fatback but would pull it out in a flurry from front and back. It was great sport, we were so caught up in the show that Aunt Lucille had Dody by the pigtail before we even realized she and Ma had arrived.

The loud screams faded as we made it to safety under the house. Billy said, "I told her that was going to happen." After a while, we could hear Dody up above us whimpering in the bedroom. We eased out into the sun to check for fleas. The hound dogs lived under the house all year round. Deciding it was now safe to join the four grownups on the front porch; we quietly climbed up and sat with our backs against the wall.

Ma said, "Well I hope you haven't been into any other mischief." I said, "No ma'am, we only went swimming." Aunt Lucille asked, "Dody too?" She and Ma looked at each other. Pa and Lonzo were grinning. My little brother felt bad about Dody getting whacked. He said, "Yeah, she can swing highest of all." Pa and Lonzo laughed out loud. Ma and Lucille frowned and looked at each other. They got up out of the porch swing and went in to start supper.

We went around to Dody's unscreened window. I was tallest but still had to roll a block from the woodpile to peep in. She was sitting on her bed looking at a movie magazine. Jon said, "tell her to come out, its all okay now." He knew she had some more good stuff to show us.

We met on the back porch and all of us told her were were sorry she got whacked. Billy said, "I told you so". Out in the shade under the tree at the tire swing, no more spinning just a slow ride now. Dody wanted to know if we had been able to buy any fireworks. Fourth of July was just a week or so away. The big tents with displays of rockets and roman candles for sale had been set up near town. Their Ma was only going to let them have Sparklers this time to wave at night. Billy's thumb was messed up permanently from the firecracker he had held too long last year.

After supper we convinced Ma and Lucille that we only needed spit baths. We told them that good swim got us cleaner than we had ever been before.

Dody slept in what used to be Grandma's room and bed. Jon and me slept in her old bed in the room with Billy in his bed.

The June bugs and mosquitoes went back out the open window and over around to the coal oil glow of the kitchen lamp. The big folks would stay up and talk over coffee late into the night.

For once, we actually looked forward to Sunday School in the morning. Billy said Dody was going to whip the tar out of a fat kid who had been teasing her. We had no doubts at all that she would do it either.

YELLOW FEVER

Even when he was small, growing up, Toody Jenkins did not have much. He lived with his Ma in an unpainted house belonging to her folks who had both died. Built by her Grandparents far enough back so the little patch of bottom and the four or five acres of hill pasture were deeded free and clear, (except for the yearly tax).

Nobody ever said anything about Toody's father. Toody had never seen him and only said he was gone someplace.

Our farm just up the dirt road was big by comparison. Really, it was about average for the farms of the area. Two hundred and eighty acres mostly woods that had been lived on and cut over for the past hundred years or more. To us, (me and my brother at ten and eight, Toody at ten), it all seemed endless.

We were lucky to have a Pa and Ma that realized boys needed a little time off now and then. There were regular chores to do even on Sunday's and of course after school each day. Saturday's unless it was hay, corn or cotton time they let us do pretty much whatever.

Toody spent most of his time at our place. With no sisters or close neighbor girls, we were totally in the dark about young females. This caused a great deal of imaginative speculation on the subjects of anatomy. Mostly though we regarded those girls, we knew from school and such with a superior sort of disdain. They couldn't do hardly any of the stuff we did and seemed to delight in getting us into trouble.

Toody got to our house as usual in time for breakfast. It was a sunny warm Saturday in late May. Pa was getting the John Deere fueled up to go disc all day. Ma was eager to set more of her little plants out of the cold frame into her garden. We would have a whole long day to work on our latest project.

Toody was very inventive, he could think up more neat ways to put old appliances or busted wheelbarrows or anything to good use.

Turning the hand cranked Blackhawk corn sheller to fill the wooden box with chicken feed was one boring weekly chore.

Toody found a rusted out swamp cooler that had been thrown into the gully dump not far from his house. The banker in town got new louvered attic fans installed in his house. The workmen had just tossed the worst of the three water drip window units away. We brought the thing home on our wagon to dismantle it. Toody replaced the corn sheller hand crank with the swamp cooler belt pulley. He nailed the electric motor on the box with the belt pulled tight, then fastened a plug in electric cord off an old hair curling iron and shoved it into the barn outlet. That thing shelled corn like never before. The empty cobs would fly out and bounce off the log wall. In just a few minutes, we had over a bushel shelled and were free to do something more worthwhile.

Ma had gotten a new Montgomery Ward washing machine. It ran off electricity too. The rural coop had brought us current about three years before. We no longer had to boil water in the big black iron wash pots out back.

The old gasoline powered Maytag with its wooden tub had been gratefully abandoned.

Toody had removed the kick-start Maytag washer motor and installed it on a cart we fabricated from some busted garden push plow wheels. Only trouble was it had no clutch or brakes. We pushed the thing to start it and hopped on, but had to snatch the plug wire off to stop. It went up and down the dirt road just fine; however, the biggest problem was fuel. We had been warned not to draw any more out of the tractors or truck tanks.

This Saturday's new project was shaping up to be our best yet. Pa and our other neighbor Mr. Bowers had worked during the winter months opening up bottom ground along the edge of the field. The big gum and oak trees, cut years ago left huge old stumps that just refused to rot out. Pa would bore a hole (with the auger used to put Hickory bows for the old holly ox yokes) into the base of the big stumps. Mr. Bowers would fill the hole with gray colored blasting powder out of a quart mason jar and put a piece of red cord fuse in about two feet long. He would then pack some newspaper tight into the hole. The powder came from the general store at town in a large tin container. Mr. Bowers stored this on a shelf in his outdoor privy and only brought a quart or so at a time. Toody knew all of this from his keen observations.

Our town water department had recently modernized by putting in fire hydrants. The big tank itself, high on the hill, was very old but fire hydrants were now required by some state law or something and were reluctantly being dug in here and there. One was still lying on its side, bright red in the green grass at the edge of town. It was on the side of the road out toward our farm. Next to the new hydrant was a pile of galvanized pipe pieces and some 3-inch parts and caps.

When Toody first informed us of this wonderful new project, it seemed like a dream come true. A cannon was the very thing we really needed most of all. Just think, in the event of another war or something we would be ready to protect our whole community. We would all three be heroes.

The four-mile trip pulling our empty wagon toward town after supper took over an hour. The few folks who passed just waved and smiled, they all knew we were often on the road. The trip back with a four-foot piece of pipe tied down with sea grass baling twine took a little longer. Whenever lights showed up we had to hide the wagon in the ditch and tell whomever it was not to worry we were headed for the house. Pa and Ma were used to us staying outside until the last minute. They only started to holler and call around eight o'clock or so in the summer time.

That was a week ago, since then Toody had slipped into Mr. Bowers's outhouse while we watched as lookouts. He scooped a jar of blasting powder out of the big tin. He also cut off a roll of red fuse cord with his pocketknife. He had to stand up on the outhouse seat to reach it and almost let the jar drop into the pit. The hardest part was drilling the hole for the fuse into the steel end cap with a hand-cranked drill. Toody knew how to re-sharpen the bit on the pedal wheel axe sharpener while my brother pedaled and I splashed on the water.

That was all accomplished during the past week, including mounting our cannon on a wheeled carriage made from an old mule drawn cotton chopper. Wired down tight with many neat wraps and pointing at an angle, it sure looked good. Just like the real ones in pictures of the war that folks could never forget.

It was fully loaded with half a quart of blasting powder packed tight, next came newspaper and small rocks (carefully selected) some nails, nuts and bolts and other ammo had been packed just forward of the paper charge. The nice red fuse was stuck in the cap about halfway into the powder and hung out the end a foot or so.

Toody wisely had fastened the carriage to a large fence post. He pointed it at a hanging molasses bucket tied from a limb in the pear tree by the smoke house.

Ma's new five story galvanized tin chicken incubator with electric heat bulbs for the little yellow baby chicks on each floor stood next to the smoke house door. Beyond that was the big heavy gate leading out to the pasture and field lot.

We had it all ready around ten o'clock or so. It was me who had drawn the longest straw. Toody and my brother peeped around the corner of the work-shed door. He had advised me to join them at the shed just for safety's sake this first time after lighting the fuse with a big kitchen match.

Ma was on the other side of the house in her garden. The popping John Deere was making a racket down near the creek in the lower field. The fuse began to sparkle and I made it to the shed door in record time. We all looked around in order of height with my brother at the bottom and me on top.

It seemed to take an awful long time and of all things, Ma was coming back around the side of the house to get more plants out of her cold frame.

It went high into the air; the whole entire cannon went straight up. Instead of a noise, it seemed at first like a quiet. Sort of a vacuum or something. The noise came as the thing started back down from a hundred feet or more up.

The incubator had disintegrated; the big gate was down with most of the post top gone. The molasses can swayed untouched. Ma had disappeared again around the corner of the house.

We realized that the priority now was to try and catch as many little yellow chicks (that were undamaged) as possible. They were dashing about everywhere. All three of us grabbed and gathered to try to put them into an empty bushel basket.

Ma came around from the other side of the house at a gallop. She helped us catch chicks and said "Good Lord", "what in the world caused the new incubator to explode!" "Are you all right? She still didn't trust electricity. We just said "Yes Mama", and tried to stand between her and the smoking busted pipe lying out by the gate. Toody was nowhere to be seen, he had just sort of vanished. Pa came up in a short while on the John Deere in road gear. He had unhooked from the disc. One quick glance told him all he needed to know.

We never tried to make any more cannons. In fact, it is rather painful to even look at a picture of one anymore. Toody came up to visit a few days later. We of course had seen him in between times, but he was kind of nervous around Pa and Ma. Especially since Pa told him he could count his lucky stars, he didn't belong to him. Ma got another new smaller incubator and we installed a new gatepost.

Toody was now working out a trap line map to set snares and traps for coons, possums and mink on the creek. He figured we could get wealthy this coming winter in the fur trade. It seemed like an attainable plan if we could get our hands on some snare cable and steel traps with our summer money. You had to give him credit he never stopped trying no matter what the downside turned out to be.

DOG HOME YET

Jan. 1945

To most folks it looked like the war would go on forever. Our battery-powered radio gave out constant reports but we had no way of telling what they meant. Rationing had the newspapers down to a couple of sheets. We were doing good on the farm all things considered. Ma was able to swap eggs, butter, canned corn and stuff for ration stamps from the town ladies, sugar and coffee stamps being the most difficult to find. Pa swapped a smoked ham and two gallon pails of sorghum syrup to the Sherriff for some 12-gauge cartridges. They were double ought bucks and came in plain olive green boxes with no other writing on them. The Sheriff received an allotment like all the other law enforcement outfits. Otherwise, cartridges had been impossible to get for more than two years. Mr. Peoples at the general store said they might never get any more.

Pa had started to let me carry the 12 gauge that winter. It was a 1914 Winchester pump and held six rounds. He only allowed me five shells at a time. The rule was deer or turkey, no rabbits, coons or possums. We could easily trap those free or use the 22 rifle for which we still had cartridges. My little brother was only eight so he carried the breech load 22 rifle.

It had snowed the night before, critter tracks were everywhere. We hurried through our chores and came on in for breakfast. I asked Pa if we could go deer hunting. He wanted to know where we thought we might find a deer. I told him there were always deer back up the logging road near the old abandoned schoolhouse. A large stand of tall virgin pines was there. Being on sixteenth section land had kept anybody from cutting them for timber. The log building itself had collapsed long ago. Pa said, "well go on then, but don't be wasteful with them double ought's."

Jon carried his single shot 22 and a hunting knife in a sheath on his belt. I carried Pa's pump gun and had a hand axe in a leather scabbard on my belt. We had on our brogans with three pair of socks. It made the laces look sort of funny. Ma wrapped some biscuits and put them in each pocket of our heavy coats. I had kitchen matches in a small Garrett Snuff tin. We drank out of the branches all year round. "Boss" our red-bone hound led the way toward the woods behind the house.

The sky looked dark with big clouds rolling all around. We reached the logging road and Boss took off in a hurry. I called him back right away and hooked a short rope leash to his collar. If he ran on ahead, we never would see anything.

It was totally quiet; the deep soft snow masked all footfalls. A few birds flew about and chirped. Some crows worried an owl way off to the West. We were headed south about three miles back into the big woods.

The wind picked up over the treetops so clumps of snow started to drop off the pine limbs. It kept getting darker even though it was not yet noontime. The snow started to fall again, just a fine mist at first.

Our plan was to let me get set with my back to a pine with a good view all down through the open virgin stand. Jon and Boss would circle into the wind and loop wide around the thickets. Deer lying down would ease on out when they caught their scent. Boss would stay on his leash to keep from running the deer. It worked just right, they had only been gone a short while when a couple of does slipped out into the open. The deer kept looking back and raising their noses up to sniff the breeze. I got a bead on the largest one at the spot behind the shoulder and slowly squeezed the trigger. She jumped straight up, and then fell down kicking. I hollered for Jon and Boss, they answered from behind the thickets. I waited and watched to see them coming. When we started back for the deer, it was gone. There was blood in the snow and some tracks going away. The other doe had gone in a different direction. Jon and Boss were out of breath. We all set off with Boss pulling hard on his leash.

The blowing snow was getting heavier but the tracks were easy to see and quite often, some red spots as well. Boss pulled free, bayed loud and tore out, rope flying on the wind. Down a hollow and up the other side, Boss was sounding further away. We ran on the trail switching hands as our guns got heavy. Now Boss sounded louder, he was barking and growling in one spot.

The deer was dead; it lay part way down a grassy hillside. The snow was falling so fast it already made a cover on the deer.

Jon held the legs apart and we dressed it out "Indian style." Leaving it on its hide, we rolled it first one way then the other to cut out the tenderloins. Jon cut the long sinew cords out of the backbone as I separated both hams and front quarters. We used the long sinew cords poked through cuts to tie one ham and one front piece together. I tied the tenderloins on my package and slung it over our shoulder to carry out.

The snow was so thick now you could only see a few feet ahead. We started in the direction that seemed right, toward the old logging road. Boss had finished off the liver and some other dog goodies but still had to be pulled along for a ways. He finally trotted along with his eye on the tenderloin. Up one ridge and into another hollow, our loads made us walk sort of slow. It was nearly as dark as night, the wind blowing hard. Even at our slow pace, we should have cut the log road by now. Things were not looking too good. Another half hour of dodging brush tops and blackberry thickets made up my mind. I told Jon, "we are going to make a camp until this storm stops and we can tell which way is home."

After a short rest, we headed toward some cedar trees with low branches like a tent. I took the hand axe to cut more thick cedar limbs while Jon swept away the snow and dead cedar leaves under the tree. We hung our deer hams over limbs as high as we could reach. The axe was great for cutting enough cedar branches to make a thick wall against the wind. The tree gave good cover from overhead. Some fresh pine straw made a cushion but it was still cold. We went out and broke dead limbs from nearby trees. When you shook the snow off, they were almost dry.

Soon a small fire was going in a pit. We put some bigger sticks, set with the ends poked in like wheel spokes, "Indian Style" again so as not to burn all the wood at once. Green hickory switches made fine roasters for pieces of tenderloin and you could hold snow in your mouth until it melted. We even had a couple of biscuits left; Boss did not get any of those.

Morning came at last, it had been a cold night but Boss slept between us and gave off a lot of warmth.

The sky was gray and clearing, the wind and snow both stopped. I asked Boss which way home, he just wagged so we knew we would need to figure it out ourselves. We had gone out south of the main road, which passed our house, and since it got light in the east, we knew how to head back north.

Pa always said when you're puzzled on coming out be sure to go in a straight line. Look way ahead, pick out a tree or landmark, and go right to it so you will not walk in circles.

We tossed our deer meat over our shoulders and set off north. I marked a tree behind us with the axe into the white bark. When we reached the one picked out in front, I looked back for a line up. We were coming out straight as a string.

Meanwhile, "back at the ranch", Ma was having fits. Pa was drinking coffee and listening to the radio. Ma went on and on asking," When are you going to start out to the boys?" He just asked her "is the dog home yet?" She said no, "What difference does that make?" Pa seemed to think that ended the discussion and turned back to his radio. Ma went to the door for the hundredth time and called for Boss. She slammed back in and said that dog is not here and neither are your sons.

Pa said, one is ten years old the other eight, they had matches and guns; there is no reason they could not spend one night in the woods. If they or Boss don't show up by lunchtime, I will go bring them back. Now let me listen to this war news.

We came out to a big bunch of beehives. They were covered with snow and being cold, all the bees were hibernating. I told Jon we might as well have a honeycomb breakfast, Mr. Bowers won't miss a few samples. We had to use Jon's hunting knife to chip the top loose on a hive. That honeycomb was some kind of good. We chewed it up and spit out the wax. I told Jon, "Better open another so we can leave some for those bees to eat." Honeycomb washed down with fresh snow water makes a fine breakfast.

It was not very far down the little dirt lane to the main road. We moved pretty fast past Mr. Bower's driveway but no dogs barked behind us. Another couple of miles and we were unloading our deer onto the back porch. Ma was scolding with tears in her eyes, Pa still sat in his chair by the radio. Later he came out and helped us salt the deer to hang in the smokehouse.

Pa was cleaning off his Winchester with a cloth and as usual putting some oil on it before placing it in the rack by the door. He asked us both what in the devil is this sticky stuff all over my gun? I said pine tar I reckon. A week or two later, after the snow melted, Pa got to laugh when Mr. Bowers told the crowd at the co-op store how a bear had tore up his beehives.

Times have changed a lot; folks would be out with helicopters and search parties if kids had to spend a snowy night in the woods today. On the other hand, not many of today's kids get taught the things they need to know to be responsible for themselves in adverse situations.

"YOU DID WHAT?"

Anybody who ever used or had to keep up a mule pulled sickle bar hay mower could tell you they were sort of dangerous.

The bar had triangle shaped blades fastened on with rivets. We would set it on the anvil in the shed to pop the old rivets out and hammer new ones in.

That bar was also spring loaded. You could turn the drive wheel to a certain place real careful. Then just a tiny bit more would cause that thing to whack through anything sticking up in it. Like a toad frogs head or maybe somebody's finger. There were lots of three legged dogs in the county back then.

Pa had to hurry up to the barn before finishing all the hay ground. A gully washing July shower that afternoon before meant it would take a couple of days of sunshine before he could cut the rest of the hay. The mower sat out in the field as we three boys walked down toward the creek beyond.

The new preacher with his wife and chubby son "Allen" had arrived in their Ford car in time for lunch. He was making the community rounds since meeting everyone last Sunday and receiving many invitations to visit.

Ma had said she thought he might turn out okay but Pa just grunted after church last Sunday.

Allen had grown up in Memphis; we had met him in Sunday school. The fact that he answered all the teachers' questions not only first but also correctly and stood up each time to do it did not impress us very much. What really got him on our bad side though was when he told his Ma about the secret knothole we had showed him on the woods side of the girls' outhouse.

Ma had told us to take him around the farm and be extra nice to him right after lunch. The big folks were going to visit for a while. Pa looked like he wished he could go with us as we set off toward the creek.

A red wing blackbird had a nest in some cattails near where the mower was parked. I slipped a baby out of the nest as we headed toward the guillotine. My little brother Jon got the trip wheel readied, I poked a twig up into the slot. "Whack", the stick popped in two pieces neat as could be. Jon rolled it back and I stuck the little birds head up through the cutting edge. Allen was crying. He said please don't cut the head off that little bird.

This was going great, better even than we expected. The plan was just to show him how tough and mean country boys were. His bawling was an added attraction.

I told Jon, okay, let's chop her off. Allen shrieked like a girl and made a grab for the baby bird.

It was too late though, the headless body flipped around on the grass. Whoops, there was something else on the grass beside it, uh oh, it was a finger. Allen could run fast for a fat city kid. We started to try to catch up but soon got our wits together and went under the house instead.

That Ford kicked up dust a mile high when it flew off toward Dr. Criss' place in town. We probably would not have been able to see it under the house, however being held part way off the ground by our overall straps as we moved fast with Pa toward the woodshed gave us a better view.

The new preacher and even Allen were nice enough to us the next Sunday. Allen's Mama was not, she just turned her head the other way while we said how sorry we were he got hurt. They stayed on for a year or two but never came back to visit again.

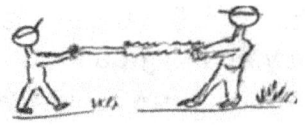

FAMILY FUN "1946"

It was a swell reunion and dinner on the ground. Folks had pretty well finished the last of the hand-cranked ice cream. My little brother and me helped clean out the zinc containers and polished off the few left over peach slices.

The grownups were all sitting down talking or slowly walking around the edges of the well-kept Evergreen School grounds where reunions were held.

Evergreen was a small one-room school with two outhouses. Inside was the one big room and blackboard. A potbelly heater stood just inside the double door entrance. Split wood was piled against the cloakroom wall. Outside under some big white oaks were three long tin-topped picnic tables.

During school times, we ate our cold sweet potatoes and poured syrup out of small Garrett Snuff cans into our cold biscuits. (The boys would have one clean finger). Most girls broke theirs in half and poured it on.

Suddenly a heavyset lady began to screech really loud. Her equally large husband was shouting, "Stay back, and stay back!" They were wealthy town relatives so my 10-year-old brother and I didn't know them too good.

The man was pointing with both hands toward a clump of sage grass while backing slowly away. Being two years older than my brother meant I was first to arrive. Other men, women, and older boys were coming that way to see what was up.

The big old rattlesnake sounded loud as he vibrated his tail from his coiled position in front of the sage grass.

Some good long oak and gum 2" x 4's had remained from constructing the picnic tables, they were stacked under the school building. I knew exactly where, as they were scheduled for night removal to be used on the tree house we had planned at home.

It was sort of like rounding the bases at full speed, first to the scene of the commotion, next to grab the board and back to commence whacking the snake, all without stopping.

We were working fast in a circle of onlookers. Some approved, others did not. A well-dressed town lady shouted loudly, "Good Lord, what are those kids doing?"

Old Mr. Snake's head was squished flat when I put my foot on it and sliced it off with my folding case knife. Next move was to the other end, the eighteen rattles disappeared into my pocket. Then back to the front to split the hide and pull it far enough back to get a double handhold on the red still moving body.

Jon knew what was expected of him, having rehearsed this recently on small garter and king snakes. He grabbed the loosened hide with both hands and dug in his heels. I hauled on the body part and just like peeling a catfish the snake turned inside out.

Attention suddenly shifted, we had lost our audience. The hefty town lady was down on the grass. Her husband fanning her with his handkerchief. The real attraction though was the other town lady who had barfed her picnic lunch on to a little girl who happened to be in the wrong place at the wrong time.

We were all but forgotten, (but not quite). I saw "Pa" headed our way with fire in his eye. He said, "This beats all!

You two don't have a lick of sense." "Get that old snake carcass off down into the woods and get back over to the pump to wash off. I will deal with you both later." He then went to try to console the large town lady but stayed clear of the other two. Jon's pocket was bulging pretty good from the rolled up snake hide. We would tack it to a board and rub salt, ashes and raw chicken livers onto it. Then after two days roll it back up and sink it in a bucket of rainwater. After a week, it would be ready to wash and dry again and would stay limber like a leather belt. That was how Indian's tanned some of their hides. Brains worked better but took too many chickens.

Pa more of less forgot about it by the time we got home. In fact, when we later overheard Ma telling him how we embarrassed her to death, he was kind of chuckling and smiling to himself.

We looked forward to next year's reunion. It was to be held at the fine wealthy folk's home in town. Their yard and gardens took up an entire block. It had a stone lined pond full of big goldfish. We could hardly wait.

TURTLE SOUP

May 1947

    Early morning, me and my little brother were walking to Evergreen School. It was a perfect spring morning to go barefoot. We had put our ankle top brogans under the bed when the first violets appeared. They would only be worn on Sundays and I would get a new pair in the fall. Jon would inherit mine; he got everything I outgrew if there was anything left of it.

    We had been warned to stay on the road, which was a longer way to school about two miles altogether. The reason was if we took the shorter route across the field bridge through the woods, sometimes we failed to arrive at all. Last week we had robbed a crow's nest in the top of a tall willow tree. A baby crow was now living in a coop at home. He had the highly original name of Blackie. Our teacher was somewhat torn about reporting our absence as she drove by in the evenings. School consisted of fifteen students' total, for grades one through six. The days we failed to show up always passed by a little easier; however duty demanded her letting "Ma" know we missed class again.

    Only a couple more weeks remained until summer vacation. The next morning, after giving Blackie his voice lessons, he just couldn't say "hello" yet, put us a bit late.

The only solution was to run fast on the field road and cut through the woods.

The creek was clear and shallow where it passed under the wooden bridge and the turtle tracks were easy to spot in the mud on the bottom. We had stopped to catch our breath and sat with feet hanging over the bridge side. There were several sets of tracks but each set just stopped with no return trails. I pointed this out to Jon who was only nine, but often seemed smarter than me at eleven. He said, "Well they just took off swimming where the tracks quit". I had another notion and went to find a long straight stick. Wading out with the mud almost up to my knees, I poked the stick down at the end of a set of tracks. Jon said, "We better go on or you know what 'Pa' will do."

The stick hit something hard so I pushed around and felt it move. Reaching down into the mud, both hands found kicking turtle feet. Out it came, a big alligator snapper, long neck and sharp jaws waving around. It landed on the bridge planking. Jon was after it fast as a fiest dog. School had suddenly become the last thing on our minds. Mr. Turtle was flipped over on his back with a large flat sand rock; several were piled up near the bridge approach, placed on his belly. Jon was eagerly hunting another long stick. I followed the next set of tracks under the bridge and out came another snapper, bigger than the first but facing the wrong way. He nearly bit my arm as I tossed him up onto the decking. Jon quickly went for another big rock. His job obviously would be securing our catch. After turtle number four landed up top, I needed a break. Turtle catching was rough work, also the creek had muddied up where the tracks were hard to see. Since we would not be able to make it to school, being completely soaked with dirty creek mud, we decided to eat our biscuits, hard boiled eggs and sweet potatoes. When the water cleared we went back to work. I brought up three more turtles. A grand total of seven now lay upside down under the rocks. Getting them to the house was going to be a major problem. Pa always said if an alligator snapper bites your thumb he won't turn lose till the sun sets and when you chop off his head those beady eyes will blink and he can still snap at a stick until dark.

Green hickory limbs coming up from a stump are extremely tough. The old folks and the Indians used them to make hoe or shovel handles. My pocket knife was not exactly sharp but finally cut enough on the long hickory pole to twist it off.

Turtle number one snapped down on the center of the limb, which Jon was holding when I poked the turtle's nose on it. We had set one end of the stick up on the bridge rail to keep it clear of the ground. All seven turtles hanging on the stick made a heavy load. It was nearly a mile back to the house so we started right off. The sun was past south heading toward west. Pa would be planting cotton in the field we had to pass by to get home.

The John Deere quit popping at the end of a row. Pa had spotted us with our long stick of turtles. He looked sort of angry at first, but when he got closer he let out a big "he-haw".

The best way to dress turtles is with a hand axe on the chopping block. Whack off their head, then two chops on the underside and you can peel the whole bottom right off. Ma brought us some pans to put the meat and eggs in. There are seven different kinds of meat in a turtle. The eggs are dark yellow with no shells. They look and are about the same size as regular chicken egg yolks. We had turtle stew, roasted turtle, fried turtle and turtle eggs rolled in corn meal and deep fried. Uncle Lonzo and Aunt Lucille came over along with our two cousins Billy and Dody. I don't think you can beat roasted turtle; it is a lot better than plain old chicken. I still dress one from time to time. Emma Ruth has cooked a ton of them over the years.

School ended a week or two after the turtle incident. It was the end of my formal education also. Jon went on to the town school to get a high school diploma. Sixth grade was it for me, but I never did regret it. Some folks just are not academically inclined.

THE FLOAT TRIP

What a fine day to hunt rabbits. The sky was bright with only a few wind torn clouds. Christmas '1947' had come and gone. A box of Super-X '22' short cartridges cost a quarter. We had each found a box in our stockings at the very bottom below the candy and oranges.

Our gun was a Hamilton breech load single shot with a brass rifled barrel. It had finally arrived after two long years of peddling Cloverine Brand Salve. We later found out that Pa had paid off and secretly disposed of the last box of 300 tins. He was under a great deal of pressure from all around the community, since we had been too good about what the sales booklet said and refused to take NO for an answer.

The temperature was in the mid-twenties, the snow dry, powdery, a foot deep in spots. Tracks of all kinds led everywhere. I was ten years old and my brother eight.

By lunch time we had reached the edge of the big river about three miles across fields and woods. There was a good place to put both rabbits I had shot them sitting in their blinds. Barges parked here and loaded out big square blocks of limestone. The quarry was cut into the bluff of the river bank. It went deep into the cliff. Back during the summer on a Sunday afternoon we had discovered long strings of brightly colored tiny copper wires. They went down into holes every few feet. We had pulled up a bunch of them to carry home and braid into dog collars and stuff. An older neighbor boy told us that wire went to blasting caps and dynamite sticks packed down in those holes. He said if we had been caught gathering that wire we would have gone to jail. This time of year the river froze almost solid so quarry work shut down until spring.

Big floats and chunks of ice were swirling by on the slow current. We left the gun on the rock shelf with our rabbits. The ice was very thick along the shore line. A huge float slid by and I hopped on it for a ride, my little brother did too. We cruised along the bank and even walked way out on the edge of the chunk nearer the middle of the river. When we started back I noticed the gap to jump across to the shore ice was a whole lot wider now. I told Jon we better run for it and hop across or we will be stuck on this float when it bangs into the highway bridge not far below the quarry.

I ran fast and landed on my backside and slid right up to the grass. Jon had just stopped, he was floating away. The gap was continuing to widen. I told him, "You better try it. I will get a pole for you to grab if you come up short." He started to cry then and said "I can't make it". I found a dead willow limb and walked along the shore ice. The gap was now about eight feet wide. I told him, "Jump in the water as close as you can get and grab this pole, if you don't I will just have to go home and tell everybody you drowned." I guess that made him angry, he backed up and hopped in close to the shore ice with a death lock on that pole.

We made it up to the corner of the quarry out of the wind. Jon was wet through and turning blue all over. There was plenty of dry sticks and leaves. A roaring fire built out a ways from the limestone corner made for a heated room. Jon stripped all the way down. I was only wet from helping drag him out. His clothes steamed and dried pretty fast on sticks around the fire.

We made it home before dark but didn't try for any more rabbits. Our final rabbit count that winter was sixty two. I think Ma got tired of fixing them. We decided not to tell them about the float trip.

THE BROWNS

Living in Mississippi, we naturally had lots of black folks for neighbors. It all seemed very peaceful and comfortable in those days. Our school wasn't much different from their school, which was located not far away.

We shared nearly everything such as truck patches, hog killings, corn and cotton gathering, cane grinding and cooking. We dressed in the same kind of clothes, attended similar small churches and nobody ever locked a door.

The Browns lived in a concrete block house by the county landfill. This was really a piece of sixteenth section school land covered with lots of deep red gullies. It was considered worthless for any school income. That was why folks several years before began to use it as the county dump.

Cornelious Browns house had been a county shop building. When the dump sort of closed in the current Beat Supervisor moved everything to a nicer location on his own farm. He installed a new metal shop building and large gravel parking area. The elevated diesel and gasoline fuel tanks were there too, right next to his own farm equipment for safety. Pa and Uncle Lonzo had some choice remarks on this situation. Everyone just said, "Oh, Well, they wouldn't vote for a supervisor that couldn't out steal them".

Cornelius Brown received free rent plus a small monthly salary. He kept the refuse from piling up in the road or other wrong places. Now and then setting the stuff on fire when paper household trash or dead critters accumulated.

The rubber tires would make a big black smoke. We always knew when the dump was being burned.

Cornelius and Camellia had two boys, George Washington and Jefferson Lincoln who were about our age. Besides caring for the dump, they ran some small side enterprises. Aluminum pots and pans, metal scrap iron, old garden tools and such were gathered into separate piles. Sometimes there would be a little copper wire or tubing. Broken furniture, appliances, sinks and heater stoves often could be re-worked to be sold from a shed out front. They also kept a few hogs, chickens and a good big truck garden for peas, greens and the like. However, their best cash income came from the Bait Shop, which was well known among fishermen for miles around. Fishing was very popular as a pastime for many town folks. Country folks seemed to stay so busy they could not go too often.

The Bait Shop was next to the road entrance; both it and the landfill had hand painted signs. Cornelius set up a box van bed off a wrecked delivery truck to keep things dry. There were half a dozen old water heater tanks cut long ways to hold minnows. Wooden ice chests sat around in the shade of the metal roofed shed made out of old car hoods.

The Bait Shop sign read "Small Minnows 10 cents a dozen, Large Minnows 25 cents a dozen, mudpuppy's 3 cents, crawdads 3 cents, red worms 25 cents a jar, night crawlers 50 cents a jar, chop fish 25 cents a bag, grasshopper's sumtimes.

Our farm had several good pools in the creek along the field edge. Cornelius and his boys snagged them out with axes and a saw now and then. That way they could drag the minnow seine stretched shore to shore. One seine would first be pulled tight across the lower end of the pool. Then they would come down from above with the other seine pulled tight from bank to bank. This caught almost everything in the middle.

My brother and me enjoyed helping (as we called it). About all we did was gather the good fish they tossed out on the shore. Pa got to keep as many of these as we could use. That was the fee he charged Cornelius for gathering minnows and other bait.

As the men sorted the fish and dressed some, the four of us, already wet, would go swimming. Always trying to see who could stay under water the longest.

Afterwards sitting in the shade, we would talk about interesting things. I asked George Washington how could he tell if his hands got dirty cause you could not see black dirt on them very well. Not in the least bit offended, since he knew I meant no offense, he said mostly you could just feel it. I told him dirt never bothered me much but Ma was always after us to clean up. He said dirt never bothered him neither but his Ma was the same way. Up at the house our Ma would have lunch fixed. Camellia and she would be drinking iced tea in the swing. The big folks ate inside at the kitchen table. The four of us ate out back on the porch. I don't recall anybody ever acting in any way out of the ordinary or regarding these visits as unusual.

Both of Cornelius boys later went to the black school in town for their upper grades. After graduating both went to a black college in South Mississippi. I gave up on school in the sixth grade. My brother made it through high school. We both joined the military pretty early and learned more about the outside world.

Whatever it was that made the circumstances so pleasant and peaceful during those earlier times seems to have all gone away. Maybe it wasn't so bad of a situation back then as some folks would like you to believe.

LESTER'S SECRET

Lester was an only child; his "Ma" took in drummers or boarders at the old hotel next to the depot. We never were too sure, why he and his Grandpa, his Mama's Papa, had the same name. He was extra large for his age, red headed and mean. He never had a father that we knew about. You never could tell if he was lying or telling the truth. He would make up a tale on some kid that sounded just right but without a word of truth in it. Our teacher caught on and quit listening to him after a while.

Lester pushed the big black rubber Navy surplus raft little Steven was underneath of. He pushed it in the way Steven would need to swim to reach the other side and come up. Craftily he stopped and waited, then slowly pulled the raft back the way it had come from.

Little Steven was all done now. He had swum and swum. He could feel the raft on his back moving. Steven had reversed to go back the way he started but was out of air and disoriented. The first big gulps of water entered his lungs. He fought to move forward and could feel the raft moving again. He screamed silently as his struggles got weaker. The kids above were bouncing and jumping around inside the big black raft. He felt them bump against his back on the rubber floor. It was the last thing he ever felt.

The whistles blew, the counselors got up out of their deck chairs starting to hand out towels. The kids grabbed the towels and ran laughing and shouting toward the cabins to change clothes. The counselors straightened up the dock area and tied the big black raft to a pier post.

I noticed Lester grinning evilly at me from his double deck bunk in the corner. It had not yet dawned on me what he had done. I had successfully made it under the raft on his dare and being out of breath had climbed the ladder onto the dock. I assumed little Steven had also made good on the dare. It was not that long an underwater swim, only twelve feet or so.

Mr. Winslow lined everyone up for the march to supper in the mess hall. Boys and girls ate together and were free to mingle at meal times. We had all gone to crafts and hobbies after our swim. I was braiding a whip out of long leather shoelaces like "Lash Larue" used.

Mr. Winslow asked if anybody know where Little Steven was. Everyone looked at each other and shook their heads, "No". I noticed Lester once more smirking his evil grin. Off we went to supper, but Mr. Winslow did not accompany us. Instead, he and another counselor set off rapidly toward the lake.

Lester came up behind me holding his empty tray on the way out of the mess hall. He whispered, "If you tell about the dare I'll say you helped push the raft". When I finally did get enough courage to tell about it, the results were not what I expected. Mr. Winslow said, "Well it was just an unfortunate accident". He really did not think Lester was responsible. After all, both you boys took the dare and nothing happened to you. Little Steven just got mixed up and should never have tried to swim under the raft. That may have been so but there would always be two of us who clearly realized it was deliberate premeditated murder.

Lester's "Ma" soon left town with some drummer. The bank took the hotel and offered it for sale. I never heard about Lester again but I often wondered over the years what else he managed to get away with.

When Baptist camp time came again the following summer, I told Pa I would rather stay home and work with him on the place. He said, "Alright, if that's what you want". He was glad to get the help.

HAPPY DAYS

Neither one of us realized it at the time, but for Toody and me this would be our last year of school. With both of us almost twelve years old sixth grade at good old Evergreen was the end of the line. Grades seven through twelve rode a bus to the town school.

We had walked to school together for nearly six years. My little brother was only nine, he would be ten when school finished the next spring. It was about a three-mile walk by road, a bit shorter across the fields and woods as the crow flies. In good weather, the woods route was our favorite. This often resulted in tardiness or even completely missed days. We had been warned to stay on the dirt road by both teacher and folks.

Being almost twelve had made a big difference in the way Toody and I regarded girls. Jon still tried to avoid them if possible.

Thirteen-year-old Lucy Ann Bowers lived on the next farm just up the road. Sam Bowers, her "Pa" raised hogs. Lucy Ann was quite plump, with bright red hair, which she wore in two pigtails, as did most of the other girls. Lucy Ann had lots of freckles and a neat gap in her two upper front teeth. She generally walked with us each day until we reached our other neighbors, the Holder girls. They were a bit younger, like my brother Jon. The group also gained one more boy, Sylvester Holder.

Sylvester was about two sandwiches short of a picnic. He had repeated all the grades starting from first. At fourteen and finally in the sixth he sort of stood out from the rest of the crowd.

One early fall Saturday Toody excitedly arrived to give us important secret information. School had recently commenced again, some three weeks ago.

The fact that Lucy Ann and Sylvester began falling behind as we all walked home in the afternoons seemed to go unnoticed. We often ran the whole distance in our hurry to reach projects we had started. Chores must first be tended to and day light always disappeared to fast.

Slipping around the side of the house out of hearing Toody let us have it. Sylvester might be slow witted but he was still smart enough to make necessary deals. Twice a month on Saturday afternoons, we each received a quarter. This let us into the town picture show, plus one popcorn and a soda. Sylvester had missed both the last two matinees, which was very noticeable since he invariably stood up and shouted at the screen.

Toody said we might want to miss this next matinee too. The deal was we each gave our quarter to Sylvester, he needed them real bad. On the way home from school just after the Holder kids turned off into their long lane was a deep cedar thicket. Sylvester would show us where to hide for a good view but we had to be very quiet.

The next school morning Sylvester met us on our way, having walked up the dirt road a little from his place. We had not said anything to Lucy Ann as she gaily accompanied us along, but Toody and I had watched her a lot closer. She went on ahead to where the Holder girls were waiting. Sylvester shouted for them to go on, we would catch up in a short while.

They soon giggled their way around a curve. We followed our guide into the cedar thicket. He said, "Gimme them quarters", you can see good from over back of them bushes".

Toody had already explained how we three were to set off running as usual on the way home from school. Upon reaching the cedars, we were to duck in, be quiet and hide. Sylvester would soon arrive with Lucy Ann. It cost him two giant Tootsie-Rolls plus a quarter each time. That was why he needed the money.

That afternoon right on schedule they pushed through the cedars into the opening. Lucy Ann giggled and squealed after dropping her bloomers, while bending over and hiking up her cotton dress. We had all watched the farm critters do this many times. The bulls and cows, hogs and even the hound dogs did it the same way.

For some reason this was different, Jon said "Wow" real loud. We were all three standing up bug eyed, watching.

Lucy Ann looked back over her shoulder and squalled. She jumped forward pulling up her bloomers and lit out for the road. Sylvester was hot on her trail hollering "wait Lucy Ann, wait".

When he turned to look back his eyes were red and mean. It was time for us to fly off through the woods toward home.

We took the field route to school for the next few days. Sylvester had threatened us at school but clever Toody told him he would be in real trouble if we let teacher or Mr. Sam know what was going on. Both Toody and me were now saving up quarters. Jon wasn't interested. Toody had sweet talked Lucy Ann so we all walked together again, even Sylvester. However, it was going to cost double. The price had risen to 2 giant Tootsie-Rolls plus two quarters each.

Our last year at Evergreen school truly was an educational experience. Lucy Ann went on to the town school the next year. Her mother took care of the new baby. Sylvester got all the credit and now worked on the Bowers' hog farm permanently.

They tried to make Toody and me ride the bus to town for awhile with no luck. In spite of threats and punishment, we prevailed. Neither of us could stand being in that town school and wound up helping "Pa" on the place.

We both joined the military when just sixteen. You were supposed to be seventeen, which we told them we were. Being large for our age must have helped as both of us went right on in.

Girls now seemed to be our main topic of interest and conversation. They still are to a certain degree, even happily married at three score and ten. Sort of like the little dog chasing the car. Whatever would he do with it if he caught it.

THE NEW TRACTOR

It was the summer we were both 15 years old. Toody and me had completed our formal education in the sixth grade. We had been pretty much full time employed the last four years or so. Our career choices were somewhat limited living in a farm community and both with a rather questionable reputation to refute. It was early summer, cotton, corn and beans needed chopping and plowing. Mr. John (not his real name) was the biggest farmer in our area. He had taken us both on earlier in the year, against the advice of his main overseer. So far, we had made him good hands. Both of us could do anything needed with a tractor and were decent shade tree mechanics and welders. The brand new red 1950 Super M Farmall was huge. Mr. John watched carefully as it rolled off the back of the delivery truck. It was the biggest tractor we had ever been around. The deliveryman gave Mr. John a package of maintenance books and drove it around in circles out on the yard. He came in and ate lunch with us in the repair shop, then left for Memphis.

Mr. John said, "Toody, I want you boys to go over to the lake place with the new tractor. Hook up and bring back that four row cultivator so we can replace some of those plows". Take it easy on this new machine, it needs to be broke in some before doing heavy work.

The lake place was a long ways off, almost 4 miles on gravel roads. This was like a special treat for us. Toody fired up the new tractor; I stood behind him on the drawbar.

The overseer gave us a bad look and said, "Mess that machine up and you're out of here."

Five forward speeds with a road gear. Toody went sort of slow until we got out of sight. He hit road gear and it was all I could do to hold on. We were flying down that straight gravel road at over 20 miles per hour.

The sharp right angle corner came up fast. Toody backed the hand throttle and punched the brake. Suddenly we both got airborne; the tricycle front new tractor plopped over on its side. Unbeknownst to Toody the brake pedal had a lever to flip down and lock both brakes together. When it was not locked, you simply locked up one wheel. This of course led to disaster.

Worse yet the thing wouldn't quit running. It spun around and around on its side in the gravel road, rotating on one big wheel. Toody tried to rush in and cut off the switch but was chased back out as the front end swept around.

All the new red paint was being scraped off the hood. We were scratched and bruised some, but the new tractor was suffering a lot more damage than us. (For now at least).

Finally, it smoked a big puff and lay still. Toody looked at me and said, "We might need to find someplace else to work".

Since it was only a little after dinner and a really nice summer day, we both decided to just take the rest of the afternoon off. We set off across the field toward the house and when we reached the creek it looked so inviting we peeled off and swam in the old swimming hole.

Neither of us was quite ready to go back and tell Mr. John about his new tractor. We figured it was better to just let things play out like they often seemed to do.

Mr. John drove up in the yard at 3:00 P.M., in a cloud of dust. Pa met him and asked what was wrong. Looking out the cracks in the barn loft let us in on the conversation. After a short time Mr. John spun dirt in the air and left out back up the road.

Toody said he guessed he would just catch up with me in the morning and went down from the loft toward his place. I sat there awhile but knew Pa was ready to hear how we had messed up again.

Surprisingly Pa was somewhat understanding. He was not too fond of Mr. John, like a number of other folks in the county. Mr. John owned the gin, among other things and sometimes there was a disagreement on how the cotton weighed out.

Toody and me did not go back to collect our small amount of wages. We agreed Mr. John might need it to fix back the new tractor and once again, Pa was glad for the help around the place.

CAMP PUSHMATAHA

Toody and his Ma, since their little spot of ground and house joined on our place, often rode to church with us. The three of us boys spent a good amount of time trying to figure out excuses to avoid Sunday school and Church. Very seldom did we come up with anything useful, although some of Toody's schemes deserved an honorable mention. Later upon reaching our early teens we found that Saturday night coon hunts or campouts on the creek helped. These could put us home late on Sunday morning. This tardiness was met with fierce threats and predictions of our being well on the way to a hot spot in the center of the earth, to us, though the risk seemed well worth the gain.

Bro. McGregor searched hard for an answer to our delinquency. Getting Ma and Toody's Mother together he had laid out a plan. He did not come right out and state the obvious but believed, somewhat correctly, that Toody was the chief culprit. The Baptist Children's Camp needed some help other than the volunteer wimpy college dudes and adventurous sorority girls as group counselors. These young folks were simply great at leading songs or holding hands in a circle with their little cabin groups. They were not, however, good at clipping the several acres of grass or riding the back of a dump truck to gather overflowing trash cans, or even washing by hand tons of dirty dishes, pots and pans.

Bro. McGregor knew that this type of work needed to be performed by husky young fellows like Toody.

The deal was that Toody received free room and board plus $10.00 per week for the camp season, June, July and August. My brother was too young to qualify and I was needed on the place to help Pa.

Ten dollars a week was big as a wagon wheel to Toody's Ma. He was conscripted unwillingly and the paper was signed. The camp was about 35 distant miles by road. We waved goodbye to Toody as he sulked and scowled out the open bus window full of little kids.

Toody shared a cabin with an old caretaker named George. Mr. George lived alone there year round to keep the place safe. He kept the water pump from freezing or other damage. Mr. George drove the old dump truck while Toody tossed the heavy trash cans up over the side. Toody got pretty good at dish washing and could finish up by 7:00 P.M. or so after the first week.

The counselor's had a cabin fixed up as a game room. It had a record player and some tables for monopoly, checkers, or cards. Toody was allowed to hang out there in the evenings but was sort of shunned by the college crowd. The half dozen wimpy boys tried hard to make him mad enough to leave. Some of the girls however would speak and seemed almost friendly. One pretty girl in particular whose name was Pepper Brinkman smiled awfully nice.

Old George took naps most afternoons when the chores were caught up. Toody soon tired of fishing for Bream. He was sharply warned about hanging around the little camp clinic ogling the red headed camp nurse. He took to visiting the counselors lounge cabin all alone in the afternoons and playing the wind up Victrola records.

It was in the second week of his hateful employment when the back door of the lounge cabin creaked open. Toody swiveled around on the couch to find Pepper Brink man blinking in the dark room. Each separate kid's cabin had two counselors. The girl's cabins were separated from the boys by the athletic field and a grove of big Oaks with picnic tables.

It was well known via the camp grapevine where Toody spent most afternoons, especially among the female counselors. Pepper had strolled in looking pretty as a picture in her camp T-shirt and white shorts. Toody leaped to his feet and hurried to cut off the sort of mushy song playing on the Victrola. It got real quiet and Pepper said "What other songs are in that stack?" She picked one out, cranked it up and got it going. It was worse than the one Toody had cut off. Toody plopped back down on the couch. There were lots of chairs but she sat down on the other end of the couch. In a short while she knew most of Toody's life story. He also received a lot of information about where Pepper was from and some stuff about her family. He had never met a Memphis girl before. Pepper was way yonder smarter than any other girl he ever knew. The record player quit, forgotten as they chatted easily for an hour or two.

The front door banged open with sunlight flooding in. Old George had come to get Toody started back on their maintenance work. Toody said, "So long" to Pepper and went to cut more grass.

By the third week Pepper and Toody were really good friends. Almost every afternoon was shared together taking a swim in the lake or just hanging out at the counselors' cabin, especially if they were alone. The hand holding period was long past; clothing was beginning to be disarrayed. Toody, 15 years old, well experienced in the most pleasurable final stages of heavy courting, had run out of patience. Pepper it seemed was not entirely a novice either. She was very concerned though about what would occur if the camp director or Chaplin or any other authority figure found out. Being almost two years older than Toody she had managed to keep things from getting overly friendly.

Toody had an old Indian motorcycle at home. He had purchased it not running for $25.00. I also had an Indian in similar condition. We were able to make both of them fairly road worthy and traveled many miles together on the gravel roads all around the County.

The weekend was approaching. Toody told George he needed to go home on an emergency to help his Ma. If you left the camp without permission you were automatically fired unless it was for a really good reason. George gave Toody his blessing and drove Toody to the bus station on Saturday. It was not a long ride on the Trailways bus. It took longer to walk the four miles out from town than the bus trip itself. Toody's Ma was glad to see him; he gave her his first two ten dollar bills and explained he needed to use part of the third one to come in for his motorcycle. His Ma wanted to know why he needed his motorcycle. He had this covered with a plausible tale. He said sometimes the maintenance department needed items from the town hardware and they would pay him extra to go pick them up.

Sunday morning during camp church found Toody quietly put-putting into the area behind the camp tractor shed. George greeted him at their cabin and said he could have saved him the walk out from the bus station with a phone call. Toody told George he came back on his Indian bike and all was fine now at home. It finally got dark; the Irish potato with a hole in it was packed into the end of the Indian's exhaust pipe. The muted popping sound was hardly audible as Toody eased out toward the entrance gate. He stood the bike on its stand and headed back in the dark to the counselors cabin.

Of course it was common knowledge by now that Toody and Pepper had sort of a thing going. The senior counselors watched them close and had warned Pepper about getting too friendly with a yard boy. They figured all was well since there was no real evidence of anything but a slight case of puppy love. The music in the cabin played while Toody answered a few questions about his recent absence on Saturday night. Pepper and he exchanged glances and he eased back out the door almost unnoticed. He was sitting on the wooden steps when Pepper joined him.

Walking toward the gate in the dark holding hands, Pepper said it would be her first motorcycle ride. She held on tight around Toody's waist as he gained speed out toward the main highway. "Ka-pow", the Irish potato blew out of the exhaust. Pepper squealed in alarm crushing Toody's ribs painfully. He explained that the sound now would continue to be much louder. The paved road was less bumpy and they both were enjoying the breeze. Toody flew past several vehicles and around a big truck or two. The moon was nearly full as they came back down the gravel road into the camp entrance. Toody cut the engine off early at a curve before he reached the gate.

He pushed the bike up into the woods and set it on the stand. Pepper had a wrist watch, something Toody had never owned. Both were surprised to find it was past midnight. They walked in very quietly and reached the dark counselors cabin first. Toody had something in mind.

Pepper protested saying she was sure to be missed by now. She needed to convince her teammate counselor to side with her on this late excursion and absence.

They sat down on the counselor cabin steps for a few minutes; maybe Toody got the upper hand. Whatever happened they soon slipped through the squeaky door and made it to the couch in the dark.

The sky was beginning to lighten up a bit when Pepper disappeared in the direction of the wash house on the way to her kids' cabin.

Toody was dozing on the front steps of his cabin when Mr. George came out to greet the day. George prodded Toody with his toe and asked, "What in the devil was the idea of staying out all night. He said the head man knew about Toody's motorbike and wanted to talk to him about it.

They fired Toody that very morning. Told him he set a terrible example for the boys and girls at the Church camp. He received another $10.00 bill and went to gather up his extra shirt and pair of jeans.

Pepper and her team mate were with their group of girls at the archery range. Toody waved while walking up. He wanted to tell her he would try to visit her after camp in Memphis. Pepper was crying, she had whispered something in her cabin mate's ear. The other girl stopped part way toward meeting Toody. When Toody got close she scowled red faced and stomped her foot. She said she knew what was going on and so did everyone else. Pepper was being discharged at the end of the week and her parents were taking her with them to Hawaii. It was no use for him to try and see her anymore.

Toody was accustomed to bad luck; he waved again to Pepper and with a sigh of relief walked out the gate.

The Indian cranked on the second kick. He had enough gas to reach the country store and service station down the road for a fill up. The trip home in the bright sunshine was great. He couldn't remember a better day. Old Bro. McGregor now was his favorite preacher; of course he never would be able to tell him why.

TOO MANY MELONS

The green GMC pickup truck was headed north toward Memphis on Highway 51. The driver had to sit up very straight and peep over the dashboard to see out. So many melons had been loaded that the truck looked like it was climbing a steep hill all the time.

Toody and I had helped to pick and load the melons. We had been paid a fair amount for our efforts before the owner set out to Memphis. The field was still covered with ripe Charleston Grays and Black Diamond melons. It looked like hundreds more were left.

With our day's wages burning a hole in our pockets, Toody zipped the black Ford coupe across the Scuna river bridge. Later, after gathering a fine supply of canned refreshments at Lasters store, we arrived back at our usual destination. Being a sleepy, hot Wednesday evening the pool room was nearly empty. The Moon players had gone for supper and would not return until tomorrow. The few regulars and other hang about social misfits made for dull companionship. They also expected us to share the rewards from our daily labors.

Toody grinned real big and suddenly popped up off the bench along the wall. He said "Come on" and started fast for the open double front doors. I knew him well enough to become rather excited. He obviously had just completed another, often marginally criminal, plan in his head.

Leaving Toody's black "41" Ford coupe parked across Front Street, I drove my old pickup truck out the dusty gravel road. Toody relaxed on the passenger side, occasionally opening two fresh cans of red neck kool-aid from the stack of cardboard cartons on the seat between us and telling me where to drive.

Back at the melon patch, I began having second thoughts. Not only was walking out of the dark field with a melon under each arm while tripping over the vines rough work, we had already done this all day long. Toody assured me we could go south to Grenada, opposite the way the owner had gone. We would get wealthy from our afterhours endeavor.

I made three trips, stopping in between each time for another can of Kool-Aid. Toody only made one trip, and then sat on the tailgate to help me unload into the truck. About trip number six, I became somewhat annoyed and told him to gather an equal amount while I sat on the tailgate.

It ended the same as always. Our long association or friendship only continued over the years because we were so evenly matched. Bloody noses, torn shirts, dusty jeans, puffing and panting, wiping faces with bandana handkerchief, we climbed in for the trip to town.

Things were quite normal as we crossed the long wooden runners of the Turkey Creek Bridge, the melons rolling about in the truck bed. As we approached the first house on the Lane road, Toody quietly said "stop". He eased out took two melons and slipped over to deposit them on the front porch of the gray house. I got the silent message without being told and did the same for the white house across the road.

We didn't run out until reaching the four way stop sign in town. Everybody got one if they liked it or not.

The pool hall was always open until 11:30 p.m. or so. The bugs whirling around the overhead lamps and falling on the green felt tables made a comfortable atmosphere. We shared our Kool-Aid and listened to the same old stories from the late night bunch.

Both of us would sleep well tonight, with a clear conscience as a result of our generosity and good deeds.

OKLAHOMA VISITOR

Naturally, it all started at the Coffeeville Pool Parlor early one rainy, June afternoon. First of the week, too wet to cut pulpwood, bored and broke we looked for Toody to provide us some Monday encouragement.

The Orville Rogers advance men had posted circulars on light poles and store fronts for miles around. Bro. Orvile's huge tent for the revival was set up on the Grenada County fairgrounds.

The three Coffeeville school buses sat idle during summer vacation. The night before we had used our Mississippi credit card to pretty well drain the gas tank on the last of the three busses.

Elwood Higginbotham was double jointed. His arms could twist backwards at the elbows. He could point his feet out sideways. Under Toody's instruction he would twist his head till his neck cords stood out and sort of roll his eyes and drool. He looked awful. Really he was just skinny. If he stood sideways and stuck out his tongue he looked like a zipper.

Toody made a crutch out of a forked cedar stick and padded the arm place with strips from a red inner tube.

Sometimes we would let Elwood sit in the middle on our nightly adventures in Toody's Ford Coupe. Elwood worshipped the ground Toody walked on. He would do just about anything we could dream up.

Off we went to the Grenada fairgrounds in my freshly re-fueled old pickup truck. On the trip down Toody coached Elwood and made him repeat it until he understood his part. I was okay with the deal until getting out of the truck and seeing the large crowd of folks inside and milling around the tent. Toody was smiling his thin lipped reckless smile. I was wishing we were back at the pool hall.

Toody held Elwood up on one side with me on the other as we shuffled through the entrance door, getting in line on the center aisle behind the disabled, many of whom were pre-paid regulars. Occasionally some teary eyed real folks would step out into the healing line to mix in with the shills.

Bro. Orvile would place his hand on their forehead, look up with closed eyes and holler real loud. "Heal, heal, Thy will be done."

When we stepped up on the platform he looked sharply at us and cut his eyes at the two big dudes in blue suits on each side of the pulpit.

Bro. Orvile did his thing on Elwood. Nothing happened, Elwood continued to twitch and drool. Toody then placed his hand on Elwood's forehead, looked up with eyes still open and screamed, "Heal, heal, Thy will be done."

Bro. Orvile sort of frowned and his two big dudes stepped closer. Elwood's head slowly straightened up, he shook one arm then the other. His feet straightened out and he handed me his crutch. Toody gave me a warning glance. It was time to make an exit back up the aisle. He snatched Elwood's shirt and headed toward the entrance shouting, "hallelujah, Hallelujah." The crowd was on their feet, clapping and shouting along with him, jumping up and down at the miracle they just witnessed.

Bro. Orvile had a smirk on his face and his hairpiece had slipped to one side. The dude at the entrance had the door blocked. He stepped aside at a wave from our two escorts who had followed us from the stage.

Elwood's recovery was amazing as we sped across the grass area to where Toody had me parked pointing out.

Our escorts held up where the cars were parked in rows. They turned back into the big tent. We flew out the sand Fairgrounds road onto Highway 8 East.

Toody said, "Elwood, you done just fine," We should all drive right on out to Hollywood. I was still rather pale and nervous. This adventure involving total strangers had been more risky than Toody's usual idea of entertainment. At least Elwood had not really required time to heal up as he had on one or two occasions in the past when we were forced to abandon him.

Back at the pool hall the tale was related over and over. It got better with each telling. Elwood was puffed up fit to bust. The word got out and many of our acquaintances crowded in. Toody took a big swig, winked and handed me the quart jar being passed around. A repeat performance was loudly demanded, so the whole group could attend up close and personal. Elwood was all for it but Toody wisely declined. He had accomplished what he set out to do. We were still broke but now commanded an admiring audience and the refreshment flowed freely. We were no longer bored on a rainy June evening.

REVENGE

June 1954

Toody had spent all night in the little lock up behind the Coffeeville Court House. At 6:00 A. M., I brought him a pack of Camels and a carton of refreshment along with a church key, (no pop tops yet). He accepted them one by one through the window bars. His backlog of unpaid speeding tickets had reached the point where "Buster", the sheriff, needed to collect. "Chester" the J. P. was set to make arrangements later that morning. I had also brought him what change I could gather, most was a loan from a certain store on the South end of town that valued him as a customer.

It was "Fatty" the Deputy who had slipped up and blocked Toody's "41" Ford Coupe with his patrol car. Toody held him responsible for the present situation.

About a week later certain things came to light. It was well known among our group that Toody always got even. Usually in ways so remarkable and inventive they would take your breath away. This was certainly one of those.

That night he had used an ice pick to punch holes in the top of the can of sardines. He had raised the hood on "Fattys" Chevy patrol car and disconnected one battery cable. This was just to keep the inside light from coming on. Working fast lying upside down on the floor board, the heater duct hose was removed. The sardine can was placed as far up into the heater box as Toody's arm could reach. The duct was clamped back together and the battery cable reconnected. Cars did not have air conditioning in those days. The heater of course would not be used for several months yet.

Only one or two days passed before all the windows on the Patrol car stayed open all the time. "Fatty" figured a mouse had died under the seat or dash board. A few days later the car was put up on the lift at Brewer's garage for a careful look underneath. The upholstery had already been removed and inspected as well as all under the hood and trunk. "Fatty" was catching heavier than usual verbal abuse from his passengers on the way to incarceration. He even gave up his normal post in his chair at the Pool Hall under pressure from jeers and nasty comments. He tried to stay away from his car as much as possible. The bad smell by now would make anybody nauseous.

Having used up the meager supply of local mechanics, (not only were they expected to perform the search for free but having "Fatty" at a disadvantage was rather rewarding). It looked like the situation would continue until nature finally caused it to dissipate.

Desperate plea's to trade it in on a new vehicle were ignored. After all it was only three years old. The previous patrol car had been a "46" model Ford which was so worn out it wouldn't even make a trade in.

The only flaw in Toodys marvelous scheme for revenge was that he had the misfortune of being a passenger on two or three occasions. Toody was tough though and bore the ride without complaint and with a satisfied smile on his face.

THE PASSION PIT

    Things sometimes got a little slow, entertainment wise, around Coffeeville after dark. Once the sidewalks had all been rolled up at 8:00 P. M., we had to look elsewhere.

    There was one special place called the "Blue Moon" on the South edge of town. It was a combination restaurant, appliance store, gas station and dispersed other items out the rear-sliding window.

    Everyone knew about this activity, the Baptist and Methodists, etc., generally sent their yard boys as they were too busy to go themselves.

    We often stopped by but presently our line of credit was stretched overly thin. The proprietor was a fine fellow but was also known for his ability to collect, one way or the other. This presented us with a choice of taking a chance on a visit or being able to fill up Toody's "41" Coupe with 21 cent regular at Brewers station tomorrow. We could not go back to touch on Herbie's crop duster at Grenada Airport yet, having just used our Mississippi credit card there but knowing we would need to purchase some gas in the morning.

    Good old Charleston was where we were headed. The new Drive in Theater was open on Friday and Saturday nights. It was against the law for it to be open on Sunday or Church nights.

We had picked Thursday night for several reasons, mainly because "Billy" who ran the projectors and sound system, would not have time to "fix things" before Friday's show. "Billy" was our friend but this was an opportunity too good to pass up.

Toody pulled the black Ford in behind the cattle shed in the vacant Fairground across from the Theater. We slipped over when no headlights shinned on the highway. The galvanized tin fence along the road, put there to keep folks from watching free, meant the gate was our easiest entrance point.

It took quite a while working fast to swap all the speaker connections. Each of us took a row, unscrewed, and reconnected by the moonlight.

Back out and across the road before midnight, we headed home, mission accomplished.

The next night was weather perfect. Having received our weekly pay let us stock up on refreshments. Settling part of our account at the "Blue Moon" reinstated our good standing.

The theater ticket girl smiled prettily at Toody. This was a special dollar-a-car load night so they didn't need the man with a flashlight to make you open your trunk. Toody drove straight to the spot way back, to the one set of speakers left un-swapped.

Billy started music playing with screened advertisements for snacks shortly before the picture began. Our plan seemed to be working okay. People were getting out of cars holding their ears. Other cars hung up the speakers to drive over the hump searching for another spot.

"You see", if your speaker was too loud you would try to turn it down. This really shut off the sound in the car next door. He in turn would dial his speaker wide open since it wasn't making any sound at all. After awhile some folks figured it out and traded speakers. Many others drove here and there to new spots. Some angry folks went to complain to Billy in the projection booth. He was totally mystified and didn't puzzle it out until the next day.

It was a onetime shot though. Billy had a pretty good notion of who was responsible. A wire pen was built next to the concession stand to hold "Killer" and "Spike", two large German Shepard's, on loan from Mitchell's Auto Parts, or as we called it, "the junk yard", next door. No more speaker switching would be attempted as they ran loose during closed times.

We quietly circled the Charleston square after the movie. Toody had installed a three quarter race cam, a set of Edelbrock aluminum high compression heads and three two barreled carburetors with progressive linkage. All this stuff along with the higher-octane aviation fuel, which made the inside of the exhaust pipes snow white, brought the horsepower up from 90 to around 130. Best of all he had put dual cutouts just ahead of the mufflers. We waved and whistled at the pretty girls sitting on cars and pickups parked around the square. This upset the boys who hollered back and gave us the universal sign language. The real reason for carefully circling the square was to see where the local law was at. The jail had sort of a branch office across from the Courthouse. Toody knew right where it was located.

He pulled the handle on the dash to open the cutouts and floor boarded the accelerator. The tires smoked and squalled, the racket rattled the Courthouse windows. The girls screamed and covered their ears, the boys shouted and tossed cans.

The getaway route lay out the South side. Toody expertly guided the sliding coupe sideways while watching the audience out of the corner of his eyes. We shot out of town toward the Payne community. The first narrow gravel road up the side of the bluff was in sight.

Toody turned off the headlamps and coasted in not touching the brakes. That way no brake lights popped on in case we were followed. He eased along making very little dust for a half mile then took off again with the usual, white knuckles on the dash for the passenger, style of driving.

After crossing the main highway at Scobey, we were safely back in old Yalobusha County headed to the house.

Next week's plans were already in the mill. It was going to take a pretty long rope to reach from the huge bell on the Presbyterian Church to the ground. Toody said how about several strands of borrowed sea grass baling twine twisted together. He was just a born genius at problem solving.

COFFEEVILLE SATURDAY NIGHT

The Indian motorcycle came flying in a cloud of dust, from the direction of the cotton gin. The rider spun around in the wide gravel of Front Street. The noise was deafening, both mufflers were removed.

Our large heavy set Deputy watched the display through the double front doors of the Pool Hall while resting in his special chair. He was being observed keenly by the regulars from the corners of their eyes. The domino players stopped their Moon game to watch also.

It was just beginning to get dark on a hot September evening. A group of teenagers, some with younger siblings in tow, formed a loose line for the movie theater next door. The Dry Cleaners on the corner had already closed.

Toody Jenkins was now back at the Gin lot. He sat on his loudly idling Indian bike enjoying the cheers and accolades. The Gin was going wide open; trailers full of cotton were parked all around.

The boys shouted "Do it again, Toody". They hoped that "Fatty" the Deputy would sail out of the Pool Hall to try and chase Toody in his "51" Chevy Powerglide.

This was not an isolated incident. Toody's reputation, which he cherished, called for him to keep the local law enforcement on their toes.

About thirty minutes earlier, across the street from the Pool Hall, a carefully thought out plan had been executed.

"Fatty" always parked his official car backed in ready to go next to the train track in front of the Pool Hall. A tall light pole, one of several, stood a car length or so behind his reserved spot.

The long rusty log chain, hooked around the base of the pole, was nearly invisible lying alongside the railroad ties. The other end, with lots of slack piled up, was hooked around the Powerglides' rear axle. Toody had been certain to get the chain off a log truck from Calhoun County. He would not have wanted to take anything from his neighbors or friends.

The movie crowd squealed and cheered as Toody made his next loud pass. He spun gravel in a circle hollering, "Hey there Fatty".

It was just too much, reluctantly the Deputy headed for his chase car. Toody was waiting, looking back from the Depot lot.

The Pool Room emptied out, all play suspended. The Chevy's motor roared, while the bubble gum machine on top started to rotate and flash red.

"Fatty" put it to the floorboard, he knew Toody would fly out of sight on highway #7, but he had to try.

Tires squealed, blue smoke rose up; the movie crowd was bug eyed. Toody had not moved. He sat looking back on his idling Indian.

The Chevy seemed to just suddenly fly backwards. The motor screamed wide open. The drive shaft had popped out of the transmission when the rear end was snatched to a stop. "Fatty" was wrapped over the steering wheel, the accelerator on the floor and the red light still flashing. Several of the Pool Room crowd made their way cautiously across the street. One reached in and cut off the key.

It was very quiet except for the popping sound of Toody's idling motorcycle.

"Fatty" raised up and pushed open the door. His hat fell out on the ground. He eased one foot out, then the other and sat sideways looking somewhat dazed.

Somebody asked if he was okay. He nodded his head and took his hat that was being held out to him. He stood up then and looked toward the Depot. Toody was grinning from ear to ear but keeping his motorcycle running just in case.

He watched as "Fatty" pulled the huge 45 caliber revolver out and braced it on the roof of the Chevy.

Keeping his reputation was one thing, but staying alive was another. The Indian flew on up toward the Gin to slide around the corner as the first loud reports were heard.

Tractor and wagon seats were hastily abandoned as the noise of something banging into the metal repair shed echoed out.

Toody caught the Trailway Bus to Tupelo the next morning. He joined up and they sent him right on to Korea. He never came back. I still have the Indian motorcycle. "Fatty" ran for Sheriff a few times but didn't make it. Front Street is paved now and the Train Depot, Pool Hall, Movie Theater and Gin as well as "Fatty" are all gone. Looks to me like the town will soon be gone too.

OLD ONE ELEVEN

Toody Jenkins was off to basic training and Korea. He sort of left me the job of upholding his reputation when he was gone. It would be tough filling those boots, but I was going to try. He had set a really great example for our small group and left us with several of his unfulfilled unique ideas.

Halloween was just about our favorite Holiday. There wasn't any store bought costumes available yet, nobody could have afforded them anyway. The little kids might wear a piece of the bed sheet with eyeholes cut out or a Cowboy hat and toy guns. They would be accompanied by older sisters and carry their paper bags around to a few places. Toilet tissue was provided free to most folks by Sears and Roebuck or Montgomery Wards. The kind they now toss into trees was not readily available and much too expensive to waste. We liked the trick part of Halloween and never looked for or expected any treats.

Old One Eleven walked with a cane. He had a white beard and mustache and like all the other old chaps whom he shared the benches out front of Baileys Store with, he chewed or gummed tobacco.

They would sit there all day to spit, whittle and tell the same stories over and over. Tobacco juice had made stains from each corner of his mouth and right down the middle of his beard. That's why we call him "One Eleven".

A big three-hole privy was located on back alley next door to the black folk's café. Each evening just before getting in his ancient Hudson pickup truck, Old One Eleven would visit it. He lived way back out past abandoned Union Hill Church on a road that no longer went through.

Four of us watched from the Crepe Myrtle bushes behind the Lodge Hall. It was a bit early to start tricks but if we waited till dark, this opportunity would be gone. The privy door slammed shut and we quietly moved forward. It was heavy but came up off the sand rocks under the corners fast and tipped right on over on the door. The muffled shout from inside was barely audible as we flew back to the bushes. A few shakes had popped off the roof and the big smelly pit was now open with the three holes pointed away from the alley.

"One Eleven" had his head stuck out the middle hole. A waitress came out from next door to look off the porch. In a short while, some men came out and slowly walked behind to see where the calls for help came from. We stayed well hidden as they checked all around. Pretty soon, a half dozen or so men set it back upright.

"One Eleven" didn't even say thanks as he hopped back toward Front Street with his cane. He got in his Hudson truck and it was two or three weeks before we noticed him in town again.

When he did resume his seat on the bench at Baileys General Store, there was a big revolver handle in his overall pocket. It was sticking out the side away from his cane. He never went anywhere near that privy though.

In fact, everybody looked around good before they went inside now. We went back to knocking on doors after setting fire to paper sacks on front porches. Most men knew better than to stomp out the fire and just kicked it out in the yard. We still caught lots of women and girls though; they seemed to not know what was in the sack and would track it back in the house to get the broom.

Paraffin jar wax or Ivory soap wrote bad words on Front Street store windows. The old timers would tell about whole wagons being re-assembled up in a tree. I guess our tricks never measured up to their standards. Lately all of it seems to be white paper streamers of tissue waiting for a hard rain to clean up the mess. Treats are now plentiful but have to be run through a metal detector, plus checked for rat poison and still are rather uncertain. The costumes are elaborate and expensive, the artificial pumpkin baskets are unloaded into slowly following (adult driven) SUV's.

You will never convince me that the "good old days" were not better and a whole lot safer.

THE COOL RIDE

Billy Brice had the first air-conditioned car I ever rode in. It was a 1959 Pontiac four door. Billy worked for a fine old gentleman named Jack DeMange. Mr. Jack owned a sawmill and the local TV cable system in Charleston, Mississippi. We put up a tower and antennas for Mr. Jack. Billy was sort of his right hand man. Billy took care of the electronics, maintenance and distribution for the cable system.

Billy was unique; there was almost nothing he didn't have some knowledge about. Hardly any factory made equipment was available then to bring in the distant TV signals from the three network stations (over 100 miles away). The few expensive amplifiers and antennas that could be purchased were only in the experimental stage. Billy made inventive improvements by trial and error that were simply amazing and improved the picture quality greatly.

One hot July day he pulled up in my yard and blew the horn, I came out on the porch and he hollered at me to come on and get in. Emma Ruth and the kids were inside, I went to the screen door and told her "it's Billy Brice and he wants me to go someplace, we won't be gone long".

The cold air hit me in the face when I opened the passenger door. Startled, I ducked down and looked inside. Billy was laughing, he said, "get in and shut the door".

He had installed an aircraft alternator in place of the regular one on the motor. He stuck a small home type window unit in the trunk along with two large truck batteries. He fed the 12-volt DC current into a 3000-watt inverter and a regular 110-volt outlet plug simply plugged in the window unit. He finished it off by running ductwork to the heater vents and cutting a hole in the trunk for the exhaust fan to blow out the back.

The car windows would actually frost up since it was such a small area to cool.

We went riding up to Pine Valley and back. He let me out in the circle drive in front of our house. I invited him in but he said no. He just wanted me to have a ride in his "cool car" and off he went toward town to demonstrate it to others around the square.

It was several years later before I owned a vehicle with air conditioning.

You could purchase kits and have them installed but they were very expensive. Billy's worked much better although you had to give up some trunk space.

(Who say's Red Necks aren't smart).

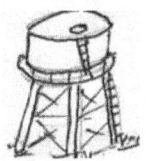

THE WATER TANK

It was along about August 1967; I had finished removing the old riveted town water tank on the hill across from the school and carried it home for a corn crib. The new water tank had just been filled for the first time. 100,000 gallons of water plus chlorine and fluoride. The pump had run all day and night to fill it up.

The call came about 5:30 AM; it was Mr. Spearman McRee, the Mayor of Coffeeville. He and the electrician had been up most of the night. The tank automatic shut off was not working and water was running down the hill behind the 7-11 Service Station. Henry Morris Lambert and R. T. Laster were both upset. The only way to stop it was to shut down the pump. Mr. Spearman said, we need you to climb up and look inside at the float, pulley, and cable. The trouble is up on top.

I headed down to town and went up the tank to see what was wrong. Sure enough, the float had risen too far and the cable was out of the pulley. When I got back down I made my report. The electrician said as soon as we put back the cable and lower the float stop all would be O.K., then he left for Grenada.

I told Mr. Spearman I would go get a long extension ladder and some rope to put up inside once the water was all drained. He thought about it a few minutes and said, no that just won't do. It cost too much money to waste all that treated water. Here's what I want you to do. Come back tonight after dark with your flashlight and pliers, (make sure nobody else knows about this). Climb up and take off your clothes and swim over and fix the pulley then come down and turn the pump back on to test it.

It was a night with no moon, inside of the tank it was pretty scary, cold water too! As I paddled across with the flashlight in my mouth, I was thinking "please Lord, don't let everybody flush at the same time". I fixed the float and paddled back, it seemed like a mile across that thing to the manhole. I stood out on the top rail and air dried for awhile, then went down and switched on the pump. It ran for some time and stopped, just right.

When I went to town to settle up the next day, Mr. Spearman said, good job, but don't ever let on how we fixed the overflow.

I think it's probably been long enough now that most of the odd flavor should be gone.

AUTOMOBILE DOCTORS

We met up with Mr. Duard Hawkins and Radford Roberts on the Elam Road just past where you turn in onto Leroy Logan's long driveway.

They liked to take off early from the Bailey Lumber Co., building crew some days for a little country riding. M.H. Harbour knew better than to try and keep them on once they had decided to go riding out to Sammy Coopers to get a couple of quarts of refreshment.

Me and Frank Murphree were in the red TVA Electric Co., truck. It was almost quitting time on a nice September afternoon and we had been trying to hide from our boss Mr. Morris McGee by riding out east of town ourselves.

I asked Mr. Duard what was wrong with his green '55 Chevy. He said it beat all he could figure out on mechanics. Radford and him had raised the hood and checked things out the first few times it quit, but now he just lit a Camel and Rad rolled him Velvet and smoked a little while. It would crank right back up and run fine a ways then sputter and quit. They were making it back to town in short quarter mile spurts.

I told him to let me and Frank have a look and we raised the hood. Duard cranked it and it ran just fine and very quiet (much to quiet). They had backed into a red clay bank when they turned about at Sammy's place. The exhaust pipe was stopped up with red clay dirt.

I broke a persimmon stick off a tree in the ditch and hollered, "Rev it up, Duard!" Rad had got out to see what we were doing. When I poked the stick in the exhaust a big puff of smoke and dirt flew out and the motor popped and roared.

I walked back around and told Duard, now you won't need to stop anymore. Rad climbed in and sat back down. He looked at Duard and said, "Well, you learn something new everyday, but I sure never knew cars were just like people."

Rad opened the other quart and offered it to Frank and me. We sampled it pretty good and headed to Mr. Morris McGee's. Rad and Duard went back to the Pool Hall.

"SCAREDY CAT"

We were living in Uncle Guy Shaw's tenant house out on Turkey Creek. The house had three rooms; both front rooms had a fireplace. I put a Sears Roebuck pump in the dug well curb out by the road. The house now had running water as well as current. I also moved the bathroom indoors. The outside one still remained for emergencies. We paid $10.00 per week rent and Uncle Guy and Vernon Vickery, his driver, arrived early each Saturday morning to collect.

Hosea Louis Dawkins, my brother-in-law had given our son, Jon, two fine black and tan puppies for a Christmas gift. They were about six months old. We built them a little house full of cottonseed next to the stone fireplace outside our living room. This was also our bedroom as the only heat came from the fireplaces and you could see out through the cracks in the wood non-insulated walls.

It was February and the coldest part of the winter. We kept the door closed to the kitchen, which was one big room across the back of the house. In the mornings, Emma Ruth would fire up the gas stove and leave the oven door open to take some of the frost out of the air.

It had started to snow about 4:00 that evening and was black dark by 5:00. The moon came up extra bright and full on the fresh snow, which was still lightly falling. With no TV and not much on the radio, everybody was reading or looking at magazines. About 8:00 P.M., the puppies began to bark. The barking got excited, then really frantic with lots of howls and yapping. I went to get my shotgun and light, Emma Ruth and Jon went to the kitchen door to peep out. The racket was back by the garden with the big woods just beyond.

When Emma Ruth turned the spinner to open the inner door both puppies came crashing through the screened door from outside. They almost knocked her over, and then stood there shivering and shaking on the linoleum kitchen floor. Boss was okay but Beanie's ear was torn and bleeding. Jon and Emma Ruth quickly began first aid, patting and quieting them down.

I eased out back with my gun ready. Something had been squalling and growling loud enough for us to hear it over the puppy's noise. A black shape sailed off the platform in the old Box Elder at the corner of the garden. Jon called this his tree house. He had nailed some boards to make a floor but no walls or roof.

The moon was bright on the new snow. The big dark shape made it to the pinewoods in two or three bounds. I had the gun up but it disappeared too fast.

It was at least a month and starting to warm up some before those pups would stay outside at night. The snow had covered all tracks by morning so we had nothing really to show. Whenever someone tells me there are no panthers in our part of the Country, I just say "Yeah Right".

HOWARD'S RATTLESNAKE

Me and Frank Murphree were riding out past Mr. John Provine Bailey's place in the red TVEPA Light Co., truck. Not much chance of our boss, Mr. Morris McGee, finding us out there. We could hide safely until lunch time.

Mr. Howard Williams was disking a field by the Bailey Hunting Lodge with a brand new Model 5010 John Deere tractor. It was the biggest tractor available at that time and was worth stopping to watch for awhile.

All of a sudden, Howard jumped off the tractor. He had not shut the motor down or anything. The tractor went on all by itself into some big pine trees and choked down and quit.

Frank and I headed out there in a hurry. Howard was circling around the tractor but wouldn't go up close. When we got near we heard a noise like a locust bug makes, only louder. Howard pointed at the dual wheels and there stuck in the mud between the tires was a very large timber rattler. He couldn't get loose but his tail and head were free. I picked up a nice piece of cedar wood, eased up and gave him a whack or two. Pretty soon the racket stopped. I pulled him out and set him on the pine straw and asked Howard what to do with him. He said toss that (bad word) thing in the back of your truck and get it away from here. Then he cranked his tractor up and went to have an early lunch.

I coiled the snake up on the hood of the red truck and drove slowly back to Bailey's store so we could go in for our sandwiches and sodas.

There was a row of benches in front of the store. The same old chaps sat on them and rested every day. When I pulled up and bumped the curb the stiff coiled snake slid off the hood and landed (still in a neat coil), on the sidewalk in front of the benches.

Mr. Mose Fly always wore white tennis shoes with no laces. It sounded like a covey of birds getting up as he went toward the gin. Another elderly gentleman named Roebuck broke Carl Lewis's 100 yard dash record as he went toward Forrest Barbers Service Station (without his cane). Runlee Robinson was right behind, his bad arm whirling like a windmill; Ob Fariss just drew his feet up with his mouth open.

I looked at Frank and said "Oh Boy", (or something like that). Maybe we better eat someplace else! I hopped out from behind the wheel, set the snake back on the hood and eased off to The Courier Office. Mr. Gerald Denley took our photo, himself, of the big old snake on the sidewalk and it was in the paper a few days later.

We got our hamburgers from Bud Lancaster at Earl McCormack's store, cut the rattles off the snake, tossed the remains in Durden Creek and went on down to Mr. Morris McGee's to see what the rest of the day might bring.

THE FLAT TIRE

Buck Durdens' wife John Eddy could fix a better peanut pie than anybody else out near rattlesnake hill. That may have had a lot to do with our wanting to help Buck get out of the sand bed he was stuck in. He was less than a quarter mile from his big old house. We were coming back from the Davis place where Hosea Lewis Dawkins was staying at the time.

The left rear tire on Bucks' 1950 model Ford was buried up in the sand and flat besides. As my boy Jon went to get the farm jack out of our truck bed we heard a loud racket and roaring from the direction of town.

Here came Bill Grayson in his cut down pulpwood truck. Bill got out without opening the door since both doors had been peeled off long ago, and looked the situation over. He had delivered another load of wood to Dub Wortham and piled it up in the middle of Front Street with all the rest of the short wood. Mr. Spearman McRee, the Mayor of Coffeeville, who also owned the movie theater, was very unhappy about the wood in the street but so far, he had not been able to get it moved away.

Bill said, "You don't need no jack, just get them taps loosened up and get the extra ready". (That's what he called the spare tire). Bill went to his pulpwood truck and got a tow sack from behind the seat and came back. Buck was still behind the wheel, he never had gotten out of his car. Bill turned backwards to the rear bumper with the tow sack under his hands and as easy as could be the whole back of the car came up in the air.

Bill had stopped by Mr. George Denleys' sliding window on the way from selling his wood and got a little pick-me-up to brighten up his day.

My son's eyes were as big as half dollars; we snatched the flat off and stuck the extra on with one or two lugs, and told Bill, O.K. set it down. He very carefully set it over out of the ruts in a new place and dusted off his hands. He wasn't even breathing hard.

After we tightened the other wheel lugs and tossed the flat in the back, Buck went home. Bill headed up the road to Uncle Marshalls'. I told Jon, that's why he doesn't have a loader on his pulpwood truck; he just tosses the logs up on top. I don`t know anybody that works like that today.

CALLING ALL FISH

The first telephone service out on Turkey Creek was a combination of private ownership and The Bell Telephone Co.

Families' of Dawkins, Harbours, Fielders, Shaws, etc., paid for and installed a single copper wire out from Coffeeville. The wire was insulated and hung on trees or poles where needed, to serve the community with an eight or ten party line.

The crank type phones, with wooden box batteries and horseshoe magnets, just like the ones in Model-A Ford cars, were purchased and maintained by each household. Later, after the phone company took over and installed the rural phone system, some people just got rid of the old crank phones. Not the Dawkins though, the old phone went under Grandma's bed in the back bed room, where it still is this very day along with the old battery radio.

Every now and then we could slip the phone out on the back porch and try to get some visiting young person to put their fingers on the terminals while we gave it a crank or two. It was great sport to see the way their hair stood straight up and to hear them squeal and holler.

One hot, late in the summer day, we decided to try a new method we had heard about of catching some of the big old yellow and blue Turkey Creek catfish. We often had good luck with our bank poles or by grabbling under the tree roots after a heavy rain, but when the water was low and clear the fish were hard to get.

Buckeye soap and green black walnuts crushed in a tow-sack also worked well this time of year, but took too much effort.

In those days Ralph Peeples store in Coffeeville sold pure copper window screen wire on big nice rolls. We got a little change together and went to purchase a piece about six feet long. We got the soldering irons, used to repair the sorghum pans, heated up and soldered the screen on the ends of two long pieces of black insulated TVA light company wire, (that used to run to Uncle Guy Shaw's tenant house). Nobody lived in it anymore.

For a good test we caught the mama house cat out of the barn loft. Sure enough, Hosea Lewis cranked fast and I dropped the cat on the screen. That cat went right straight up about ten feet and hit the ground running. We were eager to start for the creek. It looked like we might be in the, "Fish for Sale", business.

There was a big old hole, not far downstream from Mr. Parks Wilbourns' place near the wooden bridge. We tossed the screen out into the deepest part and I began to wind the crank. Up they came, small and large, little perch, minnows and several small catfish and drums. We each grabbed a tow-sack and slid down the bank. In just a few minutes they all disappeared, we only got to grab one or two. The electric current didn't kill them so they soon rolled over and swam out of sight.

What a disappointment, we needed to figure some way around it. We came up on the bank and thought awhile, maybe if I just would crank longer we would have time to gather more.

I cranked faster and hard as I could, Hosea Lewis stood with his sack ready to hop in. All of a sudden a huge yellow catfish came up. He rolled from side to side and all the way over so his round white belly was on top. He was out in the middle of the hole and slowly drifting away. Hosea Lewis jumped off the bank and nearly landed on him. He was reaching for the gills when the big old fish rolled part way back over and wagged his tail to swim off.

I hit that crank as hard as I could, a loud roar filled the air, the water sort of foamed as Hosea Lewis came up the bank. By that time, having realized my error, I was flying through the woods to put a little distance between me and that red hair. I peeped back from the safety of a large beech tree. He was busy winding the wires around the phone box and kind of muttering to himself.

He bundled it all up, screen, wire and phone, and set off across the cotton ground toward the house. I trailed along behind at a safe distance. The commercial fishing venture had failed. We would have to find another way to get wealthy.

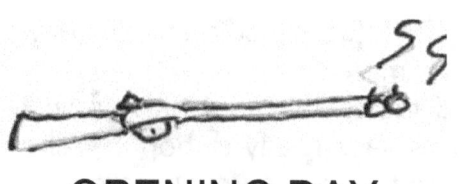

OPENING DAY

We noticed them pretty early, not quite light yet. The Walkers, Beagles and stolen town dogs were yelping and yowling a mile or two away in the cut over pine thickets. I stepped outside on the back porch and heard tires crunching gravel on the Ridge Road. Sure enough, here they came, Pickups, two red ones, a green, two white, another red, and a gray. All high up with four wheel motorbikes and aluminum dog boxes in the back. Motors roaring, a steady stream of cans, refreshment bottles and fast food wrappers flying out the windows or sticking to the juicy sides of the fancy trucks. C.B. Radios blared loud from speakers; we could hear every cuss word. It looked like a railroad train going by.

Dog and gun season was open again, from now own we would have to be extra careful while looking at fence lines, watching for gates left open, more holes cut in the wire to drag the Does out and being ready to pull off into the side ditch in a hurry to dodge the enthusiastic, reckless pursuit by the road hunters.

Five months of unwelcome, overweight sportsmen sharing their carefree lifestyle with us. Soon every wide spot will be cut up with deep turn around ruts and made into a picnic area. Yesterday there wasn't a can or bottle in sight, our neighbors' had cleaned up and down past their places and we had the roads picked up for several miles in each direction. When you live most of your life in an area with no country stores or other reason for traffic to pass by and can recognize all your neighbors on sight, it isn't too hard to puzzle out which trucks belong to the daily visitors.

My wife says the worst thing that ever happened out here was when they paved the road. I liked it better when grass grew up in the middle too.

The local Game Wardens' help a lot with the night hunters. They are doing a great job and always come over right away when called. They seem to be the most efficient and effective rural law enforcement we have at present.

Maybe someday things will improve. We certainly have no problems with the few decent hunters who actually get out of their trucks and ask permission to walk out or have a tree stand in the woods. There are four or five food plots and stands on our place and we have never had to pick up trash or fill ruts behind these hunters. It seems to be the Hunting Clubs, with large numbers of unfamiliar guests that give the most trouble.

Well it's nearly dark, time to strap on my 45 caliber revolver and make my evening rounds.

Look out stray hounds!!!! Here I come!!!

PERSIMMON BEER

Out behind the Dawkins' house by the spring box are several big very old, persimmon trees. They have been kept up and domesticated down through the past 100 years or so, the deed says from 1854. The persimmons are about the size of black walnuts and much better than the other wild ones out in the pastures.

My father-in-law, Mr. Hosea Dawkins, would make one or two clay churns of persimmon beer each fall. This year, with a house full of company, he decided to make a larger amount in one of the big black iron wash pots. He gathered a bushel or so and put them with some sugar, yeast and spring water into the wash pot. He covered it all with a clean white feed sack and latched the smoke house door. Every day after he had been out and peeped under the sack to see how it was doing. My brother-in-law Lewis and I would ask Hosea if it was ready to sample. Each day brought the same disappointing answer, "not yet".

The fourth night after supper with the girls popping corn in the kitchen and the kids playing in the fireplace room, we slipped out in the dark to the smoke house. Being clever young chaps, or so we thought, we had carried along the aluminum dipper out of the water pail on the back porch.

We carefully slipped the chain on the smoke house door and eased inside. There was enough moon to draw back the feed sack and run the dipper down the side of the pot. Gently, so only the beer could come in and leave the pulp and seeds floating. It wasn't bad, in fact we sort of made hogs' of ourselves. Later, and not near so quietly, we covered it back, latched the door and went to see about the good smell of fresh popcorn.

Congratulating each other on our secret treat, we put the dipper back in the water pail and entered the brightly lit kitchen.

There was a moment of total silence. All of a sudden all the girls and Hosea began to laugh loudly. They pointed at us and slapped each other and tears ran down their cheeks. I looked at Lewis and all around his mouth was sooty black. He had wiped his chin a few times too. Naturally, I was in the same shape. We ran fast out to the spring to try and wash up a bit. Needless to say, we had been found out.

The next morning, Hosea took the pot and dumped it in the chicken pen. It was too late to help us though. The black iron and soot the beer had picked up while working, was now working someplace else. We spent most of the next day running to the little house out back. Several times, we were thankful it was a three holer. We had accidentally discovered what they made Black Draught out of.

I never have been too fond of persimmons ever since and Lewis doesn't like them anymore either.

BIRD HOUND

THE BIRD HOUND

Renowned Coffeeville sportsmen, Mr. John Provine Dailey and Mr. Morris McGee among others were very fond of bird hunting. They kept good, well trained, expensive bird dogs and traded or up-graded all the time.

Out in the Turkey Creek bottoms in those days were lots of covey's of Quail. We called them Partridges. Many of the town sportsmen would ask permission to hunt our hay fields and pastures with the blackberry thickets growing along the edges. My father-in-law Mr. Hosea Dawkins nearly always told them go ahead and we would often accompany them.

Hosea had a 16 gauge Winchester pump shotgun which he had purchased new in 1914. That was the year this popular model twelve had come out. It was full choke, long barrel and I still shoot with it. I have never found a gun with a better feel or balance. The only problem now is the cartridges have to be special ordered.

Hosea had an old hound dog, a black and tan named Boss. He was about 10 years old at the time and went everywhere Hosea went. He could tree coons or possums or squirrels and bring them back without tearing them up after they had been shot.

This particular morning Mr. John Provine and Morris had unloaded their dogs onto the frozen ground. They got into their vests, special trousers, boots and hunting attire and set out across the hay field. Hosea and Boss followed along behind. The bird dogs ranged out, back and forth, moving fast and looking good.

Old Boss stopped near a thicket of sage grass. He looked over his shoulder at Hosea.

Hosea told Mr. John Provine, "There's some partridges in that clump". Mr. John Provine laughed politely and said, "Not likely, probably a rabbit, these dogs could not have passed that close without coming up on point."

Hosea popped the safety off the 16 gauge and walked up easy. He said, "Go Boss", a few seconds later a nice covey got up. Hosea shot one, pumped the gun and brought down another. Boss ran to the farthest one, picked it up and ran back to the other. He carried both birds at the same time and laid them at Hosea's feet.

Mr. John Provine turned red in the face and whistled up his dog. Morris walked over and did the same.

Hosea said, on down near the creek in the lower field you can almost always find another covey.

Mr. John Provine told Morris, "I think we may have better luck over on the Seller's Place." He spun around and walked fast back to the truck. Morris said, thanks for letting us hunt, that sure is some hound dog you've got. Other sportsmen came out to hunt on the place from time to time over the years. Cotton poison and weed killers made the partridges and most of the song birds disappear. We set the fields out in hardwood trees recently, which I like better. Mr. John Provine never came back to hunt again, but Morris often did. Jimmy Weeks turned loose a large number of Quail last spring. Once again we can hear them calling, "bob-white" in the mornings and see them sitting on the fence posts in the sunshine. The other birds are beginning to come back too and lots of rabbits again.

DAIRY DELIGHT

It had been a long hard day. We were late getting started from Coffeeville that morning. The tools, rope and other equipment needed to construct the Forestry Tower on Mt. Woodall, had the dual wheel truck loaded down.

The four of us were looking forward to some hamburgers and fries at the Dairy Queen just south of Iuka, Ms. We had stayed at a little motel there a week ago while pouring the concrete anchors for the new tower. The Dairy Queen was our favorite restaurant because of the neat carhops. They were very pretty and friendly. Our plan was to talk all four into a visit up to the tower site where we could impress them with our thrilling occupation.

The one lane road twisted and wound back down toward the highway to town. Everything had been unloaded up on top and it was starting to get dark enough to turn on the headlamps.

Something ran out of the woods across in front of the truck. It had looked sort of like a black and white house cat. I felt a slight bump and thought "Oh well", he has eight more lives to go.

We pulled into the Dairy Queen a few minutes later. It was as if the girls were expecting us. The boys had all the glasses rolled down; our truck was a crew cab with a back passenger seat.

The girls came rushing up giggling and laughing to the shouts and teasing of the boys.

Something however was wrong, a terrible eye-burning odor made everyone scrunch up their nose and look at each other. The vehicles on either side of us began to back out and leave. The girls grabbed their noses with their fingers and ran back toward the building. I jumped out to look under the truck, as did all three of the boys.

It was stuck up between the dual rear wheels, there was enough light to see the dead skunk jammed in tight. The manager stopped several feet away; he was very angry and waved his arms motioning for us to leave. Our carefully made plans were falling apart. Desperate to salvage something, I told Lamar, "Y'all go sit at the picnic table under the awning. I will drive the truck downwind along the road and come back.

It was all for nothing, the exciting happy atmosphere had changed. The girls no longer seemed glad to see us. We ate our burgers alone while they chatted up their usual local crowd.

The short trip to the motel was made in relative silence. It was hard to talk with a bandana handkerchief crushed over your face.

I parked a long way from the office to go in for the keys to the rooms. The lady sniffed and glanced at me sort of funny but went on and let me sign the register and pay a week in advance.

When we came out in the morning, the cars on each side of us had all been moved farther away. The people gave us bad mean looks; you could tell they had complained to the office lady.

I tried to drive fast and spin the thing out on our way to the Quick Stop store for our breakfast and lunch snacks. It flew out onto the highway okay but you could still tell what happened. People at the Quick Stop also gave us bad looks.

Up at the tower site, I squirted water from the hose into the wheels and washed the truck some. When the engineer arrived from Forestry, his first comment was "Phew".

After a week or two, we were quite used to it but it lasted much longer than that. The Dairy Queen carhops never did get to visit the top of Mt. Woodall (at least not with us).

Emma Ruth and I drove up there about a month ago. She looked puzzled when I started to laugh for no reason as we came back down the narrow one lane road.

AMBULANCE CHASERS

February, 1966

We had just left Jackson, MS, a short time ago in my pickup truck headed for Laurel, MS. Johnny Brownlee, my helper, was a Choctaw Indian and lived at the Sandersville, MS, Reservation.

The sky to the west of highway #51 south was a greenish yellow color with lots of lightning and big dark clouds. The local radio stations had issued tornado warnings off and on since late the night before. There was very little traffic in either direction. Suddenly an excited disc jockey broke in on the country music song, shouting "a tornado has been sighted on the ground east of Utica, moving toward Terry." People were warned to seek shelter right away. We had just left Terry ourselves, which caused us to glance nervously at each other.

Our line of work was constructing and maintaining tall television and radio towers. The two network stations WLBT-NBC and WJTV-CBS, licensed to Jackson were located just a few miles west of our present location. I told Johnny, "Let's ease over toward those towers; we might not need to go to Laurel today." He grinned and said, "Yeah, I never saw a tornado up close."

WLBT—Ch. #3 was a 1680" Dresser-Ideco tower. We had recently finished painting it red and white bands.

Both of us had helped to erect it a couple of years earlier when the transmitter was moved out from the old State Street Studios.

WJTV—CH #12 was a 1749" Kline tower, which we also helped install behind the county prison farm. Both towers would be in the projected tornado path.

The sky now was an eerie shade of dark green, nearly calm and a light drizzle. Both of us looked hard toward the west as we flew fast toward Channel #3, which would be the first in line for the approaching storm.

Johnny hollered "there it is!" a dancing, skipping funnel cloud with all sorts of trash and debris floating and spinning around it. I stopped the truck and we both piled out. The thing bore down on the tall WLBT tower which started to sway back and forth. Huge guy wires as big as my arm and over a quarter mile long, whipped and vibrated like rubber bands. The big red beacon lights popped and flashed blue white sparks as they shorted out. Johnny cried. "There she goes!" The huge structure lay down like an immense tree, clipping a corner of the brick transmitter building as it collapsed.

We hopped back in the truck, as the funnel cloud was now destroying an ATT telephone tower just across the road from channel #3. Red and white pieces of angle iron flew every which way. Being behind the storm, I raced the truck up the long entrance drive to the brick building. Rain was pouring down in sheets.

Johnny and me burst through the doors into the transmitter room. The emergency generator had already kicked on and the overhead lights showed "Lester, the on duty engineer, seated at the control panel. He turned in his swivel chair and said, "Hey Dave, we might need your help. I can't get this thing to stay on the air." We both busted out laughing. Lester frowned; he did not see anything funny about it. I said, "Lester, come with us and look outside, your tower is on the ground." He got ghostly pale and said, "I thought that racket was just from thunder and lightning." We walked into the back room where a hole in the roof was letting in rain.

Lester said, "There's a tarp over in the tool room, let's try to re-route the main feed lines to the standby tower. When the move was made out from town we had put the old 500" tower up near the building for an emergency like this.

I was up on top of the transmitter with Johnny holding my light and handing me tools. Lester was back at the control board so we could fire it back up on the standby.

The front door burst open again. Floyd Kinard the Chief Engineer had driven out from the offices on State Street. He asked Lester if he was alright and ran back to where we were working. It was a terrific loss and huge problem for the station and he, as Chief Engineer, was in for weeks if not months of night and day recovery work. His sense of humor prevailed however. He looked up at me and Johnny and said, "You tower men are worse than ambulance chasers. You must just drive around looking for a tower to fall down."

It was October 1967 before we completed the new 2063" tower. The NBC antenna was on top of course, but down on the side just below it we installed channel #29, the first of the Mississippi ETV stations. Floyd was forever grateful and always called on us down through the years. Several Coffeeville boys have been on top of that '2063" tower doing maintenance or repair work.

The tower fell again in 1997 when a crew from Quebec, Canada tried to replace some of the big guy wires. Three Canadians were killed in the process. We were invited to bid on what would be the fifth new tower for WLBT. The ongoing litigation and scrutiny plus new ownership made it an uninviting proposal. Besides, I had grown sort of gray headed and 2000' feet was too long a climb anymore.

MIXED COMPANY

It was 1970, early spring; four of us from Coffeeville had the job of moving a small radio station. The 250' tower, transmitter, furniture and a large record collection would be re-installed at Clinton, Arkansas just north of Little Rock, Arkansas.

We were approaching the town of Comanche, Texas, where the station was located. My three friends and co-workers were Ben Eddie Nicholson, Cornelius Mister "Snake" and Eugene Armstrong "High Pockets".

I slowed the crew cab winch truck down on the two lane highway for a better look at two road signs on the city limits. The top sign said "Welcome to Comanche, Texas", Home of the Blackest Land and the Whitest People". Below it was another sign. It read

"N—, Don't let the sun set on you here."

Now with us being from Mississippi this was not the most shocking roadside graffiti we had seen. Still this was the first time I had observed it in an official capacity on a factory made sign.

Ben Eddie turned toward me from the passenger seat, looking rather concerned, he asked, "Mr. Dave, is this the place where we supposed to work?" Snake and High Pockets sat forward on the back seat inquiringly. I laughed and said, "Well almost, our job is south of town a mile or so past the city limits".

It was nearly dark when we pulled off the highway. The Alamo Plaza motel chain reached all across the South. They even had one in Jackson, MS. Each of them had a tall arch to enter under as you approached the office.

I told the boys to duck down now, so I could get us some rooms. Snake was irate, he said, "Mr. Dave, how come we got to duck down just to sleep in this here motel?" We stayed in motels all the time in our travels without any hassle. I laughed again and said, "Me, I got to get cleaned up and catch a good rest, you three can just stay in this old truck." They grumbled but ducked down as we pulled on past the office.

No credit cards in those days, I paid the pretty little desk clerk and she gave me two keys. It was dark now and everybody was hungry. After a quick cleanup we headed out to find a place to eat. The boys ducked down on cue as we proceeded to the Dairy Queen. We would not be welcome at any of the restaurants. This was nothing new, most of the south had not yet progressed that far.

Check out time in the morning, all were rested and ready to go. Leaving the keys in the doors, I eased slowly out past the office. Nobody ducked down now. The glass door flew open and a big fat dude sailed out shouting and cussing. This suited us just fine and we all gave him the universal finger sign.

The tower removal job went smooth that day. All was loaded and ready for shipping on the trucking company floats around dark.

I told the boys, "How about we take turn about driving all night to Little Rock. We can leave this "Bubba" place to the "Bubbas". They agreed unanimously with only one demand. It was the usual request upon job completion. Stop at a Tote-sum store for ice and cokes. We kept a supply of our other refreshment under the truck seat.

There were many other incidents and adventures while traveling, "back in the day." Such foolishness is now pretty much in the past, thanks goodness.

Ben Eddie, Snake and High Pockets all have gone on to a better place. I am getting close to four score years myself and will join them soon. The first thing I will say is, "You all better duck down".

KOOL KOMFORT

It was black dark in the little wooden tourist court cabin we shared. Each of us had a bed, Lamar and me got the twin set, old John Shelton settled for a rollaway cot they brought in.

The moonlight made weak shadows through dusty cloth curtains. The squirrel cage blower fan blew a damp smelly breeze from the ancient drip box "swamp cooler". There was no air conditioning yet in homes or vehicles.

Old John was really too old for this business. We were painting some telephone company towers red and white bands again. John was in his early seventies, thin as a rail, tough as leather but mentally unstable. Fifty years of hard drinking had taken a toll on his faculties.

We were in the little town of Picayune, Ms., and had helped close up the local county line watering hole a few hours previously. John made it to his cot and crashed clothes and all as usual.

I popped wide-awake to the terrible loud cussing and banging sounds, accompanied by yips and yelps of pain.

John, being disoriented in strange surroundings, had awoken with an emergency condition requiring instant relief. The dark brown tin trashcan placed below the window fan must have looked like the answer to his dilemma. Hitting it from the side in the dim moon glow, he gave a sigh of pure bliss.

Lamar slept like a cat, the slightest thing woke him. The loud fan noise masked most sound but the warm wet spray on his face was unmistakable. We all were careful about Lamar's quick temper. Once triggered he was very hard to regain control of. John never even saw him coming. I got the light switch on and joined in the shouting, trying hard to catch one of Lamar's pummeling arms without suffering an accidental personal injury. Good thing he was barefoot or old John would have been kicked to death.

John crawled back up on his cot in a very dazed condition. Lamar was in the plastic curtained shower stall under the cold water, mumbling to himself. I was still red faced from laughing but trying hard not to let Lamar see it. The last thing we needed was to set him off again.

That morning Lamar said for me to choose who I wanted to stay. Naturally, it was Lamar, so John left for home, paid up to that day with a free tank of fuel in his old truck. We never saw old John again but heard through the tower men's grapevine that he died a few months later.

Sometimes I get brave enough to ask Lamar if he wants to find a cabin with a nice swamp cooler to stay in. He pretends to flare up but only smiles about it now.

NEW BOOTS

Early October 1959, our boss and company owner Mr. Fred Endom from Clinton, Miss., had sent three of us to Mankato, Minnesota to paint a tall 1600' TV tower red and white.

I had a new GMC pickup just purchased for $1,700.00 total price. John Brownlee and Lamar Cook from Sandersville and Utica, Miss., made up the crew.

The farther North we got the colder it got and the windows stayed up with the heater on. Lamar had the shotgun seat, with Johnny in the middle. That was because Lamar could whip Johnny and had pleasantly offered to do so. It was dark now, past 9:00 P.M., somewhere in Iowa and I was planning to stop at the next Tourist Court. No motels yet, in those days, just little wooden cabins called Tourist Courts, however it beat sleeping in the back of the truck.

Lamar and me had been rig building oil derricks in Yazoo City all summer and had each built up a pretty good amount of change. He was real proud of his new snake hide Tony Lama cowboy boots, which were sitting on the floorboard where he had pulled them off.

Johnny always chewed Red Man and he would drink Budwiser at the same time. All day and night on the way he kept asking Lamar to roll down the glass so he could lean across him and spit out the window. Lamar was trying to sleep and resented getting woke up every little while.He told Johnny if he woke him again he would make him ride on the back.

Almost an hour passed and Johnny had used the last empty Bud can for a spit can, which I had tossed out. He was needing to spit real bad and his cheeks were swelled up but wasn't about to ask Lamar to roll down the glass since he was snoring so comfortable. He glanced at me sideways and I shook my head, No. He was not going to spit across me either. He knew what would happen if he spit on the floor of my new truck. Very slowly and carefully he eased a snake hide cowboy boot over and hit it perfect center without a sound.

The tourist Court man turned on his light and gave me a key to a cabin with 2 beds and a cot. We were to tired to even build a fire in the little wood heater. It had been a long time since Johnny first started to use the new boot for a spit can. Lamar just came inside in his stocking feet and set his boots by his bed.

I always got up first in the morning and was outside checking the oil and water on the truck when I heard the terrible loud cussing and saw Johnny flying across the gravel parking lot toward the road.

Lamar couldn't run fast with only one boot on. The other was in his hand and his white sock was stained brown up past the ankle.

People were peeping out of some of the cabin doors and the manager was headed our way to see what was up. Johnny had stopped out near the road and was trying to button his shirt with shaking hands.

I was laughing to hard to talk to the manager but was keeping some space between me and Lamar just in case.

Finally Lamar hopped back inside to run tub water into his new boot and rinse it out. The air turned less blue around us and even the manager was chuckling on his way back to the office.

We picked up Johnny on the side of the road a while later. He rode on the back though out in the cold wind and watched Lamar real close through the truck glass. When we pulled in for our gas station breakfast of moon pies and soda pop, he stayed well clear of Lamar.

That night we made it to our job and settled into another tourist court. We found the package store, checked out the local action and by the time we started to paint the tower the next day, they had reached an understanding. Good thing they both wore the same size boots.

Lamar would get another new pair when we made it back to Mississippi and Johnny now had a pair just like them with one brown lining.

ASSASSINATION

Nov. 22, 1963, 12:30 P. M.

I was driving toward Dallas from Grand Prairie in the Company's 1958 GMC truck to pick up some tools and parts. The truck fuel gauge was not working; it ran out just as I came up the exit ramp onto Ervay Street. The big Texas School Book Depository was directly across the street from where I stopped at the curb. I walked into the large busy brick building. Men were wheeling carts and boxes of books in every direction. Asking to use the phone from a fellow who seemed to be directing traffic, I noticed a young chap staring at me. He stepped into the old wooden freight elevator and it disappeared on up the shaft.

My boss arrived about half an hour later with a container of gas. He gave me some money for a fill up and went back to his oil field service shop in Arcadia Park. I picked up the parts and delivered them back sometime after lunch.

The next day we only worked until noon. My friend Marshal Parks and I left for the bank at Oak Cliff to get our checks cashed.

When we came out of the bank there were police cars everywhere. The street was blocked off and people could not leave the area. Everyone was told to get back indoors right away.

The Oak Cliff theater was just across the street from the bank, the entrance completely packed with both plain clothes and uniformed cops. Shots rang out and two or three large men in civilian clothes dragged a small chap through the doors. He was cuffed behind his back; his face was bruised and swollen. They shoved him into an unmarked black car and drove away fast with all the others in line behind them.

A short while before Marshall and I had listened to a screaming babbling radio announcer. The Bar-B-Que place was packed with the lunch crowd. The announcer gave a play by play description of how Pres. Kennedy and Gov. John Conley had been shot from a third floor window of the Texas Book Depository. I tried to crawl under the table to escape the burning stares when Marshall stood up, clasped his hands overhead and cheered. Sirens were wailing all over Dallas as we drove from the Bar-B-Que place the few blocks over to the bank. Later that evening on the news the TV showed close up photos of Lee Harvey Oswald who had been captured in the Oak Cliff Theater. I told Marshall; "That's the dude who checked me out so good yesterday when I went to use the phone in the building where Kennedy was shot from".

The President had died at Parkland hospital that afternoon. Lyndon Johnson was now our new President. This made many Texans very happy. Some were not that upset about the high dollar Yankee Kennedy boy being shot.

Jack Ruby was into all sorts of money making rackets. He was known as the main hustler in the East Dallas criminal environment. My brother and I had celebrated the last New Year's Eve upstairs in his two story East Dallas club. Jack had a habit of strolling from table to table among his customers asking if you were having a good time. He would grab whatever bottle off your table and take a few swallows just to see if he could start a little something. This was well known among most of the clientele and treated as a joke. Folks would laugh and say "take the bottle with you, Jack". He had just sampled ours and moved to the next little round table. He reached out as a tall dude in a Stetson hat moved the bottle out of his grasp. Jack was not a boxer, he fought close in. They rolled about on the floor and the tall dude let out a loud howl. Jack stood up with blood all over his chin. He turned his head to the side and spit out the end of the cowboy's little finger, and then walked off.

Two days after Kennedy died Jack made the news headlines again in a photo on the ramp coming out from under the downtown Police station. It showed him with a gun in his hand being wrestled to the ground by some large Marshalls. He was such a frequent visitor to the station that nobody paid much attention, not until after he shot Lee Harvey from four feet away.

Jack's cell was carpeted and had a nice soft bed and easy chair. He sat in front of his private color TV. He mysteriously died of a heart attack some weeks before he could testify at the congressional hearings.

I was living in a duplex apartment place in Grand Prairie. My boss said two plain clothes men had come to the shop while I was gone out on a job. They wanted information about how long he had known me, where I lived and other stuff. The next morning a telephone company truck had parked across the street from the apartment. The repairman put up a little canvas tent on the pole to keep the sun off while he worked. It stayed up there for a couple of weeks.

Out at the local racetrack, where my friend, B. Y. Gardner and I drove super-modified race cars on Saturday nights there was a rifle range. The tall race track embankment made a neat place to set up targets. For a nominal fee folks would practice or adjust scopes or shoot pistols. Mr. O. L. Nelms was a self-made millionaire. He owned the track/range and a big Army-Navy surplus store. He waved his finger in the air and called me over to where he sat in his special chair. He weighed over 300 pounds. He said some plain clothes marshals had asked if I used the range for target practice. He said he told them not that he ever heard about. I just drove a race car for Mr. Preston Long who owned Long Van Lines, a moving service.

Nothing ever came of it; they never actually questioned me about anything. It did show how thoroughly they followed any lead on who may have helped Lee Harvey shoot Kennedy and the others.

I left Dallas to come back to Mississippi that spring. It was a strange set of coincidences to have been right there among all the activity. Most likely there were dozens of other people checked out during the investigation, including all the Book Bindery employees.

I still believe both Oswald and Ruby had their mouths permanently closed to protect the real perps from being identified. 1963 was an unusual year.

THE ROYAL GORGE

It was early May 1965; our boss "Fred" had phoned us as we completed a contract in New Orleans. We had just finished painting the tall radio tower on top of the Jung Hotel on Canal Street red and white again.

I was driving Cecil's new blue Ford pickup truck; Lamar was smoking a Roi-tan cigar and sipping on a Dixie beer, a cold twenty-four bottle case sat on the floor boards between his boots. Each of us had decided to have a Dixie breakfast to celebrate our exciting and most welcome new job assignment.

Cecil seemed a little nervous, as I passed everything on the two lane road while maintaining a steady 70-80 miles per hour. Not many interstate highways yet and traffic was heavy on old 90 West. Lamar was totally relaxed as usual. The radio blared out country tunes and all the truck glasses were down. Life just couldn't get much better.

Fred had wired, by Western Union, our payday for the Jung project. This new assignment at KOAA-TV north of Pueblo, Colorado would be a real money maker.

The antenna on top of the 1050' tall Blaw-Knox tower needed repairs. They also wanted the angle iron tower repainted while out there. When these big network stations had a major problem the priority was immediate retention of broadcast quality. Fred was extra good at taking advantage of this situation. Years of experience and smooth salesmanship got us top dollar, also the competition in our line of work was almost nil. The insurance coverage was astronomical.

About lunch time, Lamar tossed the last empty Dixie bottle off the mile high bridge at Lake Charles, La. I pulled into a Gulf station to fill up one tank and let us drain another. Lamar came out with a cold twenty-four bottle case of Lone Star beer, since we now would be driving through Texas. Cecil purchased three large bags of salted peanuts, one apiece. With lunch out of the way, it was back out onto the race track.

Cecil would drive his truck after we reached our destination and all around the job site, he always had me or Lamar drive the long hauls. Sometimes it caused him to swallow an entire chew of Beechnut tobacco, but either of us could maintain a 70 mile per hour average cross country on two lane roads.

Lamar's driver's license had long ago been revoked, however he still carried it. Mine was under a lot of pressure but not yet invalid. This was in the days of tube type radios, no computers, so in most places we just paid another ticket, (which Fred grudgingly covered).

The station engineer was overjoyed to welcome us and expected instant progress on this antenna problem. After twenty some hours of high speed travel with a beer only diet we were somewhat less eager to make the climb. I consented to go up for an inspection trip just to keep things friendly. Upon reaching the antenna in the last bit of daylight the problem was easy to spot.

The steel galvanized elements had fractured from wind vibration or metal fatigue.

They would need to be re-welded. This would eliminate the ghosting and flickering picture image on everyone's screen.

Cecil told Mr. Renfro, the engineer, what the nature of the problem was. He also asked about the nearest hotel and gave him a list of materials to be ready for us in the morning. The engineer went ballistic and shouted he was going to call Fred. Part of the deal was no delay in getting this repair completed. Cecil replied in his slow Mississippi drawl that we would need to rest up a bit and if that didn't suit him to call somebody else.

The KOAA signal was restored to full quality shortly after lunch the next day. A regular welding torch would not burn properly at that altitude, above 12,000 feet although the tower was only 1050'. I had used a device that burned pellets which made oxygen and brass welded or brazed the elements back in place.

Mr. Renfro was ecstatic; he was now our new best friend. He called all the neighboring radio and TV station engineers in the vicinity to tell them an A-One tower crew was in the area. Soon Fred received phone requests from three or four other local stations to have us perform repairs, light bulb changes and re-painting. This often happened, in the early days, when we worked in Montana or Utah or somewhere less traveled.

On a sunny Sunday morning, about two weeks later while still in Colorado, Cecil drove us out to have a look at the tallest bridge in the world. Sundays were reserved for a little R & R unless it was an emergency situation.

Lamar had a cold case of Coor's beer between his boots. He tried to stay with local brands, but his Roi-Tan cigars never changed. We had finished KOAA-TV as well as both AM radio towers and looked forward to a new destination in a couple of days. Pikes Peak seemed to be on a level straight across from the top of the KOAA-TV tower.

Rounding a curve on a twisting mountain road a Colorado Highway Patrol car met us. Cecil always drove very slowly. The blue lighted bubble gum machine on the patrol car suddenly lit up. The trooper spun around squealing his tires as he pulled in behind us. We all got out to see what the excitement might be.

The trooper was very young, probably not much out of his teens. He asked Cecil for his license, standing up close and directly in front of him. Cecil had been taken by surprise. His mouth was full of Beechnut tobacco juice and he was trying to smile. He spit a stream, about a half a coffee cup full, at the ground. The wind blows all the time in Colorado and most of the tobacco juice went on the little trooper's shiny cowboy boots. Cecil smiled real big now; he reached in back of his overalls pulling out a red bandana kerchief and waved it in the air then bent down to wipe off the trooper's boot. The trooper had put his hand on his gun butt, his eyes were big and round. Cecil straightened up and drawled, "Sorry 'bout that son. What was it you stopped us for?"

The trooper stepped back holding Cecil's license. I thought he was going to cry. He asked, "Are all of you from Mississippi? What are you doing out here?" Lamar had a Coors in his hand and was puffing on his cigar; I was turning red in the face trying not to bust out laughing.

Cecil said, "We come out here to fix KOAA-TV and you folks seem to want more stuff done. What was it you stopped us for, son? Can I have my permit back?"

The trooper looking stern again, back in charge handed Cecil his license. He asked, "Do you realize your windshield is cracked?" A stone had flown up and hit it several weeks ago, the crack had spider webbed from one side to the other. Cecil said, "You bet son, I fully intend to get that thing replaced soon as we get back to Mississippi! Can you tell us if this is the road to that tallest bridge?"

The trooper was scratching out a ticket on his pad. He handed it to Cecil and said you must get that windshield repaired right away. You can pay this fine at the courthouse in Pueblo. Cecil accepted the ticket without looking at it, folded it and put it in his overall's pocket. He said, "You still never told me if this is the bridge road!" The trooper frowned as Lamar took a swig of his beer. He said, "Yes this is the road, about four miles ahead." He spun on his heel and walked to his patrol car shaking his head. We watched him whirl back around again squealing his tires as he went on his way.

It was a tall cable suspension bridge with a wooden deck. People were strolling across it taking camera shots of each other and the scenery. Cecil parked the truck and we stopped walking out in the very center. Down below a railroad train was passing; the cars looked like tiny match boxes.

Lamar told Cecil, "hold my beer", handing him his Coors, he climbed over the rail and disappeared beneath the decking. His head popped back up and he told me, "come and have a look at how this thing is made." I promptly handed Cecil my beer, which he tucked under his arm and climbed over the railing after Lamar.

The cables were not large, only 1" or so and laced across with other smaller cables all held together with cable clamps. We crawled around under the bridge and came back up on the opposite side. A large crowd had gathered, looking at where we disappeared. Two men in white aprons and an old guy in a uniform were running over to that spot. Cecil stood there with three beers waiting for us to report back up. One of the dudes in an apron shouted at Cecil. "What are you trying to do out here? Where did those men go?" Lamar and I walked up behind the group. I said, "Hey Cecil, we're right in back of ya'll".

Cecil ignored the dude in the apron, he handed us each our Coors and asked, "What did it look like under there?" Lamar said, "Well not too good, a lot of those old clamps are rusting pretty bad, they need to be changed out." Both men in the aprons seemed to perk up at that statement. Other people were taking our pictures. The tallest one said, "Who are you boys? Where are you from?" Cecil replied, "We're from Mississippi, out here on a job". The short guy in the apron asked Lamar, "How rusty are those clamps?"

Well it turned out they owned the fancy restaurant across the bridge and also owned the bridge. They asked us to come over for a free dinner and talk some more about the condition of the structure.

We spent the next week under that bridge replacing clamps. Made more off that deal than what Fred owed us for our regular work. Cecil had called and told Fred we would be out of pocket for a few days, we needed a short vacation. Fred fussed and gripped, but moved our next job Florida up a in Jacksonville week or so.

It was kind of neat working on the tallest bridge in the world. Cecil got us out of there in a hurry though, soon as he collected. I had suspected it and Lamar couldn't have cared less, but those two restaurant dudes were more than just good friends.

Jacksonville, Florida was nice; we installed a new channel 11 antenna on the local 1500' tower and visited Jacksonville Beach each evening. Fred found out about the bridge and told us we owed him for extra motel and travel but he never collected.

I would not take anything for the memories of those days as a nomad, drifting back and forth across the country without a care in the world. I often wonder who it was that took our places.

"SUPER BOWL, MAYBE"

This is a true and accurate account of an incident that nearly caused one of the first Super Bowls to not be televised.

Our boss in Jackson received a phone call from an extremely agitated Chief TV Engineer in Denver, Colorado. This was in the earlier days of television when the signal from the "on site" cameras had to be transmitted via the local main distribution antenna and transmitters. Other stations could then re-broadcast simultaneously, to be viewed by the entire country.

This call had come in on Saturday; the game was to be played the next day. The station KOA-TV was having transmission problems. A local man had gone up the 1000' tower and found burned sections in the copper feed lines, but he was unable to make a repair.

Lamar Cook from Utica, Mississippi, my helper, and I boarded a private Lear jet for a very fast trip to Denver. There was only the one pilot besides us so I asked if it was okay to sit up front. He said yes, but don't touch anything. That little plane went straight up, then leveled off and in what seemed like no time at all dipped down at Denver.

We had our climbing gear, tool belts, wrenches and pliers in canvas bags along with a pair of extra jeans and socks. Many of our jobs were away from home and often overseas so we kept a kit ready at all times. They had told us to bring cold weather clothes.

The Engineer was waiting in a station vehicle. He actually ran out to meet the plane. On the way, he explained what they thought had happened. Someone had shot a hole with a high powered rifle into the large copper line way up close to the top around 800' or so. These lines are pressurized with Argon-Nitrogen gas to prevent the signal from arcing or shorting out. When the gas escaped several joints of 20' sections had burned up.

We put on our warmest clothes, gloves and our headlamps, like coon hunters wear. It was 3° below zero and snow everywhere on the ground. I asked the assistant engineer how they could even play football in these conditions. He said no problem, the field was covered with big tarps and folks just bundled up to watch the game.

The tower ladder rungs got bigger as we went up. Ice had formed on them, so after 500' or so our hands would no longer reach around the rungs. We continued up by hooking our arms over each slippery rung. I got Lamar started removing the bad pieces leaving him at work and going back down for the stuff we needed to fix the thing. Upon reaching the ground, I was met by a large group of men, broadcast managers, advertisement dudes and the engineer who was bordering on a heart attack from the pressure of not being able to televise the game.

I told him come with me somewhere warm where I could give him the list of what we needed. Like most stations, they kept a long drum of nylon rope and pulleys along with spare sections of transmission line. He had anticipated the biggest part of what was required and even got the local supply man to deliver extra cylinders of Argon gas.

Back up the tower I went with a pulley block and the end of the long rope. Lamar was using his little come along to pull down against the spring hangers and already had removed and tied off a couple of bad pieces in the corner of the tower. He was so cold though he could hardly talk. I tied the end of the rope around him and sent him down to warm up.

The engineer had slipped a WWII walkie-talkie over my shoulder so we could talk back and forth. I had already told Lamar to tie three new pipe joints on the line at ground level. In turn three bad pieces would be tied on up top, this would act as a balanced counterweight with new sections coming up as old went down requiring very little pulling effort. It worked pretty well and all the new pieces soon arrived. We both worked hard until dawn shined a cold gray light over the mountains.

We came down to an even larger crowd of men shouting angry questions and demands. Both of us were too frozen to pay any attention and went into the transmitter building to find a radiator and thaw out. I told the engineer to pressure the system and then let it bleed back out a couple of times to remove most of the oxygen. He pressured it as we watched the gauge. If it held it meant no leaks, if it dropped off, we would need to go back up which I was not sure either of us was in shape to do.

The line held and the transmitter went on at low power. The VSWR or signal reflection was higher than before but acceptable. Full power was applied and at

8:30 A.M., the Super Bowl could once again be viewed all across the country.

The station manager, chief engineer and the owner's representative were ecstatic. They had a car ready to take us to the Holiday Inn where breakfast and a fancy room were waiting. For many weeks, there had been no rooms to be obtained in Denver. Someone had been prevailed upon to vacate this one just for us. We also had an invitation to sit in a heated box and view the game.

Neither of us had the least bit of interest in football. I asked the main man if we could load up and get a ride back. He looked like I had just spit on his shoe or something. He said yes, if that was what we really wanted he would call and get things set up.

I had to sit in the back on the way home. This time there was a co-pilot as well. Both those dudes acted somewhat grumpy and it seemed to take longer going back to Jackson. They had given up their game seats and would miss the pre-game party because of us.

It wasn't all bad though; Lamar found a little refrigerator full of Jim Beam and Jack Daniels in tiny bottles with Coke-Cola and ice cubes. What we didn't consume en-route went into our tool bags for later use.

Our boss gave us each a thousand bucks for our part in saving the Super Bowl. That meant he kept three for himself since I had overheard the engineer on the phone talking before we left.

I have yet to watch a football game. Looks to me like a bunch of oversized dudes in tight pants running into each other while another one scampers around on the grass with a funny shaped ball.

They do this for a couple of hours and everybody gets real excited. I prefer watching Tony Stewart pilot his Chevy at 200 plus miles per hour into and around other cars as he racks up a million dollar purse. He has won over seventy million total in ten years of racing, all without chasing a ball of any kind, round, egg shaped or orange. Different strokes for different folks.

OUCH" THAT HURT

    Our line of work kept us constantly on the road in a new place every week or two. Retaining a happy redneck crew meant locating a suitable beer joint or honky-tonk nightly at each new destination.
    I had a small 32-caliber revolver loaded with starter pistol blanks. The kind coaches used in those days for track and field events. The thing looked real and it fit well in the top of my boot wrapped in a bandana kerchief.
    It seemed like more often than not some local honky-tonk dude with his reputation to maintain would get peppy and say something ugly. This was expected and generally looked forward to as enjoyable nightly entertainment by my merry group of three or four.
    Usually I would just watch and let the festivities reach their normal predictable outcome. Most times, they all wound up being best buddies with a whole new set of friends. Setting up the house meant the bartender and girls would be eagerly awaiting our arrival the next evening.
    Once in a while though things would go awry. The starter pistol made a very loud "Pop" when fired into the air and never failed to get everyone's attention. All would be well again when it was laughingly explained it only contained blanks. I kept it in the truck glove compartment while traveling from tower to tower.

Melvin was missing that morning when the others staggered out of the motel rooms on their way to get coffee and breakfast. Not quite ready to abandon him in this small West Virginia town, I asked who had seen him last and who he went off with.

An invitation to a poker game on the second floor of an old red brick warehouse was too good to resist, especially when it was tendered by a giggly, chubby little barmaid.

I left the boys at the Waffle House and drove our crew cab winch truck where instructed, trying to track down Melvin. He was walking up the side of the road when we spotted each other. Jumping in the passenger side he angrily exclaimed, "We got to go back up there". It came out in the questioning that he had given up his wristwatch and I was going to have to advance him $50.00 to get it back.

I explained this was not going to happen, pulling over while looking in the rear view mirror to make a U-turn. The next thing I felt was a poke in the ribs. Melvin had grabbed the starter pistol out of the glove box. He was whining about how that watch had been the only thing his Papa left him.

Continuing my U-turn to head back toward the rest of the crew must have been what pushed him over the edge. Of course, a night of beer with whiskey chasers not yet eased off by black coffee also contributed.

"Bam" our eardrums nearly split. The paper wad hit my shirt and powder burns made a brown hole. It hurt like the devil. Melvin's head banged the windshield hard when I mashed the brakes totally from reflex. I snatched the little pistol from his hand and he bailed out onto the ground.

In his confused angry state, I was supposed to be rapidly becoming history. He had forgotten the little gun held blanks. Still on all fours when I rounded the truck, he was a sad sight.

Pressing the pistol against his ribs, smiling into his face I watched his eyeballs pop wide when the thing went "bam". He hollered "Ouch" real loud grabbing his side. I shoved him into the cab and slammed the door. We both were laughing about it when the story came out while eating our waffles and bacon with the others.

That was Melvin's last trip out though. When our boss heard my complaint, he agreed to get rid of him.

We met him again a couple of years later. He had joined up with a tower crew out of Nebraska. It was a poor rag-tag Company of misfits and ex-cons and he fit in great. They only did small nickel and dime jobs. He begged hard to come back in with us but nobody wanted him around anymore.

LONG PIG

October 1966: We arrived in Boston late at night in our crew cab truck, loaded with tools and equipment, ready to construct a tall television tower on Bunker Hill overlooking the city.

As customary while on the road, a steady supply of beer and whiskey was mandatory. Upon reaching each new destination the first priority was locating a suitable bar or honky-tonk near our cheap hotel and job site, one where we could establish a rapport with the waitresses, management and maybe clientele.

At 2:00 AM the choices were limited. One area near the wharfs stayed open 24-7. We deposited our gear in a seedy hotel. A short walk found us in an old fashioned tavern. It was a long brass railed bar just a couple of doors down the street from our new home. Two drinks in the dis-mal, dark, smelly, lonesome atmosphere decided our next move. The nightly routine seldom varied, stay out and drink until the wee hours. Find a place to eat a steak or a couple of burgers, stagger to bed, wake up with a bad head and locate some coffee and donuts.

The nature of the work took care of our previous nights excess quite rapidly, the extreme physical exertion and constant subliminal knowledge that your next few breaths could be your last, soon shaped us up. 3:00 AM arrived; Lamar needed a steak before sacking out. The dim lit street showed only a single neon "open" sign.

Red flashing tubes outlined the entrance to a Chinese Pagoda style restaurant.

Up the steps and in we went, the only customers in a large dark room. Small round tables ringed a center table with six chairs. We sat down and waited. A red curtain opened, a little bushy haired Vietnamese slid out holding four menus. With four beers ordered we attempted to read the list of entrée's. The creepy little dude brought the beers on a tray. Each of us ordered steak with rice, since no potatoes were offered. Another little dude looking like a twin was scowling out the curtain slot with bright black eyes. His scowl, no doubt, a result of the loud profane, abusive manner in which our orders had been placed.

Black eyes and facial smirk gleamed evilly as the next round of beers was distributed one by one. The odor of meat cooking drifted out, accompanied by subtle muted laughter and oriental gibberish.

Dinner was served, each individual slice of steak sat alone on small white plates. Rice came in a large communal bowl, to be distributed into smaller bowls.

The meat looked more like ham; it was thin cut with an odd grain and texture. More grayish red colored like a rare slice of fresh hog.

Lamar dug in with his usual gusto. Cecil and David complained about plain old rice while heaping their bowls. I cautiously cut off a tiny bite and chewed it slowly, tasting for identification. The others were beyond taste testing. Huge gulps of beer washed down bulging cheeks full. I noticed the gleaming bright eyes peering out the curtain slot. They seemed to be bursting with merriment.

"Holy Crap", it dawned on me in horror stricken realization. I spit the un-swallowed bite out; my chair fell over backward with a clatter. We often found ourselves in awkward or out-numbered situations as we toured those degenerate watering holes in various places around the country.

No matter how inebriated they happened to be this type of loud shout or reaction from any one of us triggered instant alarm. It set off a conditioned response in all of them. Lamar was on his feet in a flash. Cecil and David swiveled around with eyes squinting to identify the source of danger.

The watching black eyes disappeared. I moved fast toward the entrance waving an arm for the rest to follow. Puzzled expressions but painful past experiences made for unquestioning, immediate obedience. One little Viet had a machine pistol in his hand, standing behind the check-out counter. He was shouting pay the bill in broken English. I already had a twenty out of my pocket and tossed it on the counter in passing.

We hit the dark street running flat out for a couple of blocks. I stopped to answer a puffing, panting, bewildered babble of questions.

My own puffing brief statement, "Long Pig", was met with silent odd stares. Suddenly Lamar busted out with a big belly laugh. This confused Cecil and David even more. Lamar then revealed the source of their latest scrumptious repast. He said it was probably the butt cheeks off a recently deceased Viet local. Those folks made their own mortician and funeral arrangements.

Cecil and David retched and vomited. I felt queasy but had not swallowed any. Lamar continued to laugh. He said he would just as soon eat a gook as look at him.

So much for fine dining in Boston.

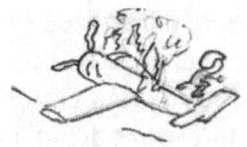

SPOOKY AIRCRAFT TALES

May 1954" We were making our landing approach to the carrier Intrepid CVA-11 on heavy seas in the North Atlantic? Our AD-4 single engine fighter had dual yokes, (we sat side by side). The young Ensign pilot had only come aboard a week ago. The LSO flagged us off just short of the fantail. We were low and fast. The kid shoved the yoke forward and chopped the throttle on the 3350 cu Curtis Wright radial. The tail hook popped off along with part of the fuselage. The landing gear almost popped up through the wings. Bouncing back airborne we drifted forward toward the Davis Barrier. This was a straight deck, no options, aircraft parked up forward. I watched as the starboard wing peeled off on my side when we contacted the island. Men were scattering everywhere. We spun into the net in a bright orange ball of 115-145 av-gas. The kid was frozen in place trying to talk into his mike. I blew the canopy, slapped his helmet and rolled out chute and all into the fire and foam. The hose boys hit me with a load of foam and I crawled away toward the back of the plane. I wiped enough off to see the Ensign whirling across the flight deck on his back. The monster in the asbestos suit we called (Hot Suit Harry) had reached in and bodily tossed the kid out of the plane. The medic told me to come down to sick bay for a shot. I responded saying the last thing I wanted was a shot and I was going to get a shower. The foam is made from soybean oil and cows blood. The medic of course won out, in sick bay he handed me one of those miniature bottles of Jack Daniels. He said, "That's your shot". I told him it looked like I needed two shots; he reached in a cabinet, smiled and gave me another bottle.

Later back in the red lighted ready room, filling out the mandatory stack of paperwork, the Squadron Commander asked if I would be interested in some shore duty. This was my third crash in the past two months so the decision was fast in coming. I got sent to Dallas, Texas NAS test facility, the field next to Chance Vought Aircraft Co., home of the Corsairs and Crusaders. It was real choice duty. We made touch and goes on a painted simulated flight deck, I could sleep through the whole deal. The guy that invented canted deck carriers deserved to have one named after him.

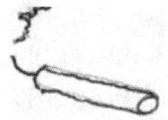

FOURTH OF JULY

Sam Tidwell and me had a serious fender bender on the sand road in front of Isaiah Brown's house. It totaled both his 1955 Ford and my 1960 Ford. Mr. Milton Tackett sold me a nice yellow 1961 Olds to replace it. My boss Mr. Morris McKee at TVA gave me a few days off.

We drove on down through the back to Meridian and over to the Alabama line. A brand new Stuckey's restaurant, gift shop and Texaco station was there and Emma Ruth and Jon wanted a banana split ice cream and soda pop. The first thing Jon noticed when we entered was two huge tables of fireworks of every kind, piled high, halfway to the ceiling.

Sitting at the ice cream counter, I watched as three young chaps came in. All had short hair and black Navy type military shoes but wore civilian clothes. They were about half snookered, pushing and shoving and giggling. The tall one lit a cigarette as they walked down the aisle. He looked down and touched the end to a double red string of what we used to call "penny fire crackers". Then laughed and shoved his pals toward the front door. The owner was already coming around from the cash register, but they popped out and ran past the gas pumps.

Jon and Emma Ruth were enjoying their banana splits when World War II cut loose behind their backs. The owner was on the telephone now, the two counter girls ran screaming for the kitchen. Most of the many customers just stood still with their mouths open, big eyed. I snatched Jon off his stool, grabbed Emma Ruth's hand and we flew out through the kitchen after the girls.

Once outside I gave her the car keys and said take Jon, don't rush, move the car up on the service road and come back to that grass place over on that little hill. Then I ran back inside. Red, green, yellow was bouncing off the walls; smoke so thick that nothing but the flashes were visible. I hit the floor on my belly, about two feet of air remained. A one legged man was huddled down in a corner his crutches lay this way and that. I bundled him up, ran and pitched him out on the grass. He rolled over twice; sat up and said get my crutches. On the way back in, I thought, "Boy that's gratitude." I tossed the crutches out the door and went down on my belly for another look. High heels and two fat ankles about ten feet ahead. I hauled on the ankles attached to a fat lady in a dress and out the door she slid. I stood her up, dusted her off, she was dead quiet, scared, totally speechless. Her husband was with a group of yelling people about one hundred yards off. Nobody came forward; I pushed her in their direction and started back in. No way; solid smoke and fire now, Jon and Emma Ruth were shouting and pointing. I looked around and saw bloody arms and hands waving out of two smaller windows up high in the block wall. Burglar bars had them covered. Jon came when I motioned, he was only 8 years old. I told him go with Mom, get the bumper jack out of the trunk and bring it here. He ran like a deer, Emma Ruth could too in those days. I pried the bars off a window and out came a black guy feet first. He hit the ground moving. A large white man was standing on the commode trying to get out. I caught his belt behind his back and peeled him out on the ground. While prying off the next set of bars an elderly bald man came out of the crowd to help me. We took two little girls and their mother out of the men's room. The other men had been in the ladies. I walked over to where Jon and Emma Ruth stood, apart from the now large crowd.

All the other nice cars in the lot were burning. They all could have been moved. The people stood and murmured like a flock of sheep. The gas pumps were going good out front and everybody needed to be a lot farther away. That was enough for me, I picked up Jon and the jack, told Emma Ruth let's go. We drove off without looking back. We met half a dozen flashing fire trucks and police cars on our way toward Meridian.

About 20 miles West on old 80 highway, we stopped for something to drink. Dr. Pepper and moon pies for them and a cardboard six pack and nickel church key for me. No pop tops in those days. As we pulled into the small service station, I noticed a young chap standing by a white 1964 Chevy. He ducked his head but looked familiar. As we made our purchases, the other two punks ran out, jumped in the car and flew off.

Yup, it was them again. Auto tags were big in 1968, only five digits, easy to read. As I came back inside, the owner looked at me in a funny way and asked "Do you know those kids?" I said yeah, can I use your phone? You could still borrow a store phone then too. Looking up highway patrol I asked for the dispatcher saying could he please take some information about the fire on 80 East. He said they were already aware of it but go ahead. After getting the story about the kid touching the fireworks with his smoke, and the car color and tag number, he asked "Who is this?" I hung up.

We got some gas and fell in behind them on our way to visit Emma Ruth's sister and my Mother in Jackson. About two and a half Buds later, a bubble gum machine on top of a patrol car was flashing blue lights. There they were, pulled over, pocket books on the hood of the Chevy, all three shaking their heads and arguing. The Trooper writing in his pad, nobody noticed us as we eased past with the traffic. Jon was reading a little kid's book. I said, "Oh well", the Stuckey's man will never forget their faces. We drove on into Jackson.

The Sunday paper had a big color aerial photo of the fire. The underground tanks had gone up. The article went on to say fortunately there were no injuries, no mention of how it started.

Emma Ruth told me to write about it. We have never really talked much about it in the last 36 years, but it was a very memorable Fourth.

STREAKERS '1970'

Dayton, Ohio was a big busy town. The television tower we were painting red and white again was located next to a well-kept city park. A large green hedge ran alongside the boulevard street beside it. A nice college was located across the park just a block away.

The songwriter Ray Stevens from Nashville was very popular that summer. His song about "Don't Look Ethel" played several times a day on most radio stations. He either had started or was taking advantage of this new odd form of adolescent rebellion. Streaking was currently increasing in frequency among young folks, much to the delight of my tower construction crew.

Just after lunch, three boys and two very attractive girls had walked across the park area and were giggling and laughing right under our tower. The thick hedge shielded them from the boulevard traffic. When they began pulling off their clothes, Lamar hissed at me and pointed down. We all sort of hid and stayed quiet. The young folks never thought about looking up so high.

One boy gathered all the clothes and set off down the inside hedge toward the corner a couple of blocks away. The others peeped out through an opening, watching the traffic, as they got ready to jump out and dash down the sidewalk to slip back in and get dressed where their clothes were waiting.

My boys thoroughly approved of this neat activity. When they popped out of the hedge and began their run a tremendous cheer accompanied them from above. All four slammed on the brakes in confusion, and then spotted us waving and shouting from overhead. After a few seconds, they waved back and tore on down the street to pop back in at the corner. Car's had stopped passing and some drivers had gotten out for a better look. It was a great success enjoyed by all.

We faithfully watched for them every day the rest of the week while we finished the 600' tower. For some reason though they never came back. It really was the high point of our Dayton, Ohio job and would always remain a fond memory from that trip into Yankee territory.

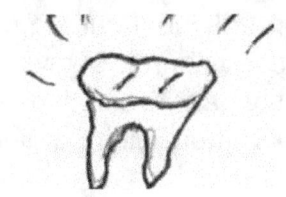

JUNGLE DENTIST

We were living in the little Central American Country of Belize, just south of Mexico. I had a contract for twenty-two communications towers for the Belizean government. Our new house was on a big river several miles back in what was called "the bush".

My jaw was swelled up pretty good. The local dentist was more of a veterinarian. He ran a few head of cows and pulled teeth on the side.

Karl draped a not too clean towel across my shirtfront and handed me a quart of white rum. Since this would be the substitute for Novocain, I gulped down as much as I could before coming up for air. White rum was generally not used for drinking. Regular brown rum was much cheaper. The locals called the clear white stuff "dead man's rum". That was because they used it to wash down bodies before a viewing. It sort of helped with the air in the room in this tropical heat too.

Karl stuck what looked like a pair of water pump pliers in my mouth. I never knew the pulling of a tooth would make such a terrible racket. He pulled, waggled, and got all red and sweaty. My lip was bleeding pretty good where it got pinched. We both took another swig on the white rum. Karl emptied the bottle.

Back to work with his knee in my chest. My ribs hurting more than my jaw now. "Got her", he shouted falling back into the wall. He proudly held out the red tooth for me to see. It had little spongy chunks of jawbone stuck to it. He rinsed it off in a rusty pan. We both inspected it closely.

Karl said "Shucks" there ain't nothing wrong with that there tooth.

I stuck my finger in my mouth and felt the bad one with the hole in it. He had just pulled the tooth in front of it.

Karl said "Well we done come this far we might better get'er done". The idea did not appeal to me but the logic was sound.

Karl opened another quart of white rum, swallowed a big part and handed me the bottle. When I set it down half, empty it was pink rum.

I drooled and gargled while Karl got a good grip on tooth number two. He had about as much of my gum in his pliers as he did tooth. It popped out fast since the one in front was already gone. He plopped it in the pan and said "Now that one is worth five dollars".

He did not collect; I hit that door in a hurry, jumped in my truck and sped off down the sandy narrow jungle road for the house.

Emma Ruth put up with my groaning and moaning. She even got me a quart of regular brown rum, not the burying kind.

I saw Karl a few days later at the ferryboat crossing. He sidled up to me and said "What about my five?" I told him as much enjoyment as he got out of that mess up he was lucky I didn't take five dollars out of his hide. He just laughed and said "Well don't come to me next time you have a bad tooth". I didn't have a reply to a statement that dumb.

MARTIAL DUTY

August 30, 2002—"Hot"

The mall opened at 10:00 AM. We stopped near the main entrance, Lincoln's, Cadillac's, and Mercedes outnumbered the Ford's and Toyota's.

Rotund senior citizens were gathered in a cluster, walking shoes and towels around their necks. A hefty black woman security guard unlatched the doors. The odors of fast food, greasy sausage, coffee and pastry poured out, along with a blast of cold air.

The regulars crowded in, sat down on green plastic benches, twisting sideways to slip on expensive sneakers, tuning up headsets, checking side mounted odometers, off they went. Waddling seriously down the half mile of tile on the right and back up on the left, past the elaborate fountains spraying chlorine water under stained glass skylights.

My wife had paused at the directory booth just inside to locate the most lucrative shops and sales, enjoying newfound companionship with half a dozen other coupon holding, enthusiastic, bubbling, female shoppers. She quickly pointed out the bookstore on the grid map and advised me to stay right there until she arrived with her plunder later in the day. Soberly I glanced about at the three or four other lost and bewildered husbands, those who were designated as bag toters looked back in raw envy. Not pressing my luck I started immediately for the bookstore.

Strolling along amazed and fascinated at first, on down the length of shining floor, keeping close to the wall out of the main stream of puffing grayish blue hair and varicose veins. I saw absolutely nothing I needed or wanted. The clothing was ludicrous, the gift shops inflated, East Indian jewelry vendors, new automobiles, and stuffed animal booths were set up in the median. Loud, illegible, horrible tunes blared out of video and so called music stores, in odd conflict with elevator music playing softly from overhead speakers. Everything seemed to be made of bright colored plastic, including the food items displayed under glowing glass cases.

Tobacco smoke, and often-another popular type of smoke, drifted on the artificial breeze from gaudy, profane T-shirt shops, racks of billed caps with nasty messages or motorcycle emblems hung on the entrance trees. Obese, bored, young sales persons lounged on sofas and chairs, drinking and eating from huge Styrofoam containers, occasionally glancing away from their TV's at the passing, heads up, walkers.

Suddenly I was aware of being physically nauseated, from the ambiance and atmosphere, not just the sights and sounds and odor. It was the thought that this place is representative of America's values. A czar like excess never before equaled, a daily ongoing, increasing symbol of waste and foolishness, the perpetual squandering of resources, along with a seemingly total absence of morales, integrity, or responsibility. This shallow ignorant society was snowballing toward disintegration, a vain thoughtless quest toward some hedonistic utopia.

Like a diver who has descended too deeply, I tried to walk carefully, slowly, out the nearest exit, just to see the sky, even if through the big city layers of pollution and exhaust. I wanted to put my hand on the trunk of a tree, to get off the concrete and imitation marble for a while. With a grateful feeling of relief I pushed out of the gigantic, claustrophobic enclosure and breathed in the warm humid diesel scented air.

Later, mentally refreshed, I braced up and headed back into the ritzy bookstore.

Finally, my wife arrived with dangling bags of expensive, unnecessary, temporal purchases on both arms. The third phase of the shopping excursion was about to begin, phase one having been the queasy, rather frightening 60 mile, early morning drive over. Our next joyful move, for her, will be visiting a high priced eating establishment to ingest some tasteless franchised lunch, while maintaining a smiling face.

I secretly knew that the rude, baggy eyed waitress with the silver bead in her nose had just come from the restroom with unwashed hands. I also could see the large, dark, tattooed cook sweating busily into the powdered mashed potatoes. I just knew he used heroin nightly to offset the last stages of AIDS. I mused that perhaps something like a nuclear strike would pleasantly occur, before our next dreaded Xmas shopping trip, looming up on the refrigerator calendar. All the while trying to locate a clean place to sip some of the swimming pool tasting water between the greasy fingerprints on my glass.

Phase four was about to begin, the 60-mile return trip. A dangerous and deadly gauntlet of vicious, harried 3:00 PM drivers, tailgating and constantly darting out to pass on the double yellow lines of the two lane highway, cell phones in hand, radios blaring, they fly in both directions. Desperate to reach their next destination. School busses signaling the end of their few hours of weekday freedom and licentious adventures.

    At last my heart rate begins to slow. We are only a few miles out now, back in familiar surroundings. Maybe, God willing, another dutiful marital chore will soon be over, my frozen smile can be abandoned, and "Hooray" here comes my dog to meet me.

YOU REAP WHAT YOU SOW

Imagine a vast pristine land of diverse climates. Exactly as God made it. Unchanged, inhabited by a vigorous, disease free, honorable people. A people who bathed each day, breaking holes in the ice in winter, drinking quantities of water and keeping a goose feather to put down their throat so they might start each day clean, both inside and out. A people who lived for thousands of years in such harmony with the environment that they could move from locale to locale and in a few months all would be as if they never were there.

Imagine shiploads of debilitated, vermin ridden, bad smelling people, rapacious, degenerate, whose most handsome men and women have yellow, ruined teeth from their unwholesome diets of salt pork and wheat flour, paid to leave a land of plagues, confusion and starvation. A dishonest people, professing to worship a God, yet treacherously wicked and deceitful in their dealings with each other and whomever they met. Whose first act upon reaching new shores was to locate and loot the Natives granaries. Being observed unmolested by the Natives who assumed they were starving to commit such a dishonorable deed.

In less than three hundred years this falsely pious, self-righteous, horde of mixed Caucasians, Africans, and Asians occupied the pristine land. They devoured, spoiled, poisoned, and polluted, virtually all the native creatures and plants. Cut down, burned, wasted, virgin forests, slaughtered millions of Bison, passenger pigeons, waterfowl, netted the plentiful fish for fertilizer, wiped out many other species for skins, fur or feathers.

Committing steady, lying, purposeful genocide and unspeakable atrocities on the original twenty-two million inhabitants, deliberately exposing and infecting the Natives with smallpox, cholera, venereal diseases, etc., People who had no immunity, all the while declaring how the heathen were being saved and converted to a superior life style.

Becoming a world power from the unceasing exploitation of seemingly endless resources. Even now, reaching out to all parts of the globe and beyond. An unbelievable, constant, insatiable greed, always under the guise and delusion of wholesomeness and pure religious conviction. Quoting clichés about democracy while every day killing and maiming hundreds of innocents in poor deprived countries. Using high tech missiles and advanced weaponry on people that still travel by donkey cart. Most of whom cannot even point toward the USA.

This greedy, obese, self-righteous people who call themselves "The Great Society", are without doubt the most wasteful, decadent, evil, consortium ever to occupy a space on the planet. Consuming the very earth itself at a horrific pace. Burning unnecessarily, billions of gallons of fossilized fuel each day. Probing into the last remote areas of unspoiled territories with ever more sophisticated larger, faster machines. A single cross country flight by jumbo jet distributes more unregulated, noxious waste into the atmosphere than a small town would create in a week. The huge fuel powered generating plants, massive half mile long super tankers, millions of heavy trucks and personal vehicles. The list is endless. All these so called modern necessities, invented, developed, created either by or the results of American's heedless quest for toil free, luxurious, existence, (regardless of consequences) undeniably affirm the USA as the catalyst for worldwide Armageddon.

The lifestyle of American inner city dwellers makes Sodom and Gomorrah pale in comparison. Government taxes pay for preschool and adolescent Ritalin or narcotics, cloning experiments, and abortions on demand, making puree of the unborn to be injected into the bodily systems of eccentric octogenarians who possess uncountable personal fortunes.

Noah took 500 years to launch the ark. Babylon and Rome each lasted several hundred years. Their bad behavior was a mere ripple on the pond compared to the abominable present day rate of American consumption, destruction, vandalism and desecration. Do you know of a rural Church or Cemetery that has escaped graffiti, trash or burglary? The oceans, rivers, lakes, huge land areas, even large portions of the atmosphere are being ruined hourly.

Cities, Urban communities and their governing political entities are an absolute sewer of corruption and favoritism. Convicted drug dealers and users elected as mayor of the nation's capital. (I.e. Marion Barry). The U.S. presidency after Clinton is a pornographic joke. So-called prime time television advertises Viagra and similar sexual stimulants during supper. Explicit sexual acts are a normal part of the accepted titillating, evening viewing.

Any form of deviancy, filthy language or perversion is considered harmless and amusing by those who have usurped the airwaves.

Marijuana is grown and distributed, crystal methamphetamine cooked and sold openly in rural communities everywhere. Mississippi alone now has over 80 gambling casinos in operation. Tax money pays students to learn the gambling trade in our Universities and Schools.

The public education system is a mismanaged, pathetic, billion-dollar enterprise. Controlled by grasping ethnic, political zealots who's only real goal is personal profit and hedonism. Check out the Mercedes and Lexus in the D.C. parking lots.

Schools in small communities have State and federally assisted budgets in the hundreds of millions of dollars yet continue to produce illegitimate babies from equally bastardized teens. Spilled out delinquent and illiterate with diplomas into the welfare system to make a living out of the mailbox, like those before them have done for some 35 years now.

The thousands of tall buildings and skyscrapers across the country contain people shuffling papers or punching keyboards, producing no legitimate product. Their livelihood being derived from the diminishing few workers who actually do produce something, who are struggling to extract a living for themselves and families from the soil or sea, while taxes take up 60%-80% of their earnings. In turn, used to support the lazy undeserving who purchase fine vehicles and items from abroad, where manufacturers still are able to control quality.

The real reason people from the world over come to the U.S. illegally is as always, unchanging. In America you are permitted to worship the Occult, Baal, Voodoo, any known or pseudo religion is allowed. You may frolic in the groves; everything is permissible and free indeed, if you are of that mindset. Mexico, among others, has no equivalent State or Federal welfare system. No food stamps to trade, no WIC, no ADIC, no self-induced disability payment, not even three free school lunches plus transport each day. No other place but the US offers these myriad, crippling, self-defeating entitlements, which are really government programs administrated with massive profits for select groups of bureaucrats and politicians. Paid for with taxes from others unfortunate enough to responsibly own property or farms.

The USA is at a peak right now. The world's only super power. The biggest Roach's on this round popcorn ball, gobbling up and excreting at a rate never equaled or even imagined. Devouring each other or anything in the way, while naively puzzling over some desperate chaps from the Middle East, who are willing to commit Hari-Kari, just to make a statement about Americans leaving their land and way of life alone.

Deja vu, Mohican's.

Most likely God has already begun another project, another world, where only the type of folks who originally inhabited this country would be welcome. He may resurrect a few exceptional souls from the current ongoing meltdown. But whom have you personally known, past the age of accountability that met the biblical criteria of goodness or kindness and qualified for eternal life?

It's difficult to believe that our Native American predecessors are continually burning up someplace because they never had access to the word as compiled in the Old and New Testaments.

The Native Americans mostly believed in one God, "The Great Spirit", and realized that everyone was going to meet him eventually.

The vitriolic, profane chants of the new rap music, performed by disgusting, nasty mongrels. Bodies pierced by bits and pieces of plastic, only lacking bones in their noses. Stoned and smoked, drunken and numb, these are the most influential, the revered, dominant leaders for our youth to mimic and fawn over at raves and concerts. Where thousands gather weekly to wallow in drugs and perversion. No innocent lack of modesty here, rather lewd exhibitionism and nakedness.

AIDS infected tall green haired or bald semi-literate, rude, athletes are paid huge sums of money to dash about after an orange rubber ball, to hang by one arm from a net. While other gibbering fools in grotesque costumes eat, drink, slobber and scream profanities at each other. Groups of equally oversized; dull witted giants, in numbered shirts, grunt and push to move an elliptical ball around on the grass, to the delight of obsessed crowds of decadent, surfeited, obese, pampered millions.

It is certain that only a few more years of resources remain for this aberrational blink in history called America to continue. Mushroom clouds will begin to appear, large scorched portions of earth resembling the sand and rock craters of the moon will be the landscape.

Perhaps the moon and other planets once looked like ours. God must have learned more from this particular brief experience in husbandry than any other. Maybe heaven is just his next effort at a better creation, hopefully populated by the spirits of a people who once lived here undisturbed.

Eve set things in motion across the sea. God has admonished the people of that hemisphere again and again. Perhaps there was another Adam and Eve for this country, since people here were never bothered much about wearing clothes, nor were they ashamed to be without them, until the falsely pious, unwelcome newcomers destroyed their innocence and way of life.

Possibly God's plan was for the two different society's to meet and assume the better qualities of both. However, human nature always seems to gravitate downward, as evidenced by the current ever-accelerating decline of society in general. God may yet chose to salvage what little is left of his beautiful creation. But my guess is that he long ago decided to do as it is written. Make All Things New.

There is one word that accurately portrays our present day Western philosophy, "Denial".

TRULY, YOU REAP WHAT YOU SOW.

WORKS CITED

Henderson, E. (n.d.). *Proud And Free.*
Seattle, C. (1854).

PROUD AND FREE
There was a people proud and free,
They stood beneath the sky,
They danced and sang upon the wind,
They watched their spirits fly.
Mother earth did give them life,
They dwelt on her with care
Taking, always giving back,
To cherish what was fair.
Standing tall, strong, and brave,
They walked in harmony,
With nature and her boundless gifts,
A people proud and free.
(Henderson)

One thing we know, which the interlopers may one day discover, our God is the same God. You may think you own him as you wish to own our land; but you cannot. He is the God of man and his compassion is equal for all. This earth is precious to him and to harm the earth is to heap contempt on its creator. The new Americans too shall pass, perhaps sooner than all the Indians. Continue to contaminate your bed and you will one night suffocate in your own waste.
The earth does not belong to us; we belong to the earth.
(Seattle, 1854; Henderson)

EPILOGUE

If this life had treated me any better I would not have been able to stand it. The highest points may be mostly behind us but every new morning is thankfully viewed as a fine adventure for the two of us to enjoy.

Somehow, time, circumstance and geography all just combined. I have no choice; I must enter the ethereal with a smile on my face.

BIO

Born Minot, North Dakota, 1937, moved south at age 8. U.S. Navy C.A.C., 1953-1956, two flight deck crashes; Douglas Skyraider fighters. Worked out of Mississippi 1956 until retirement; as lineman, rig builder, tall steel tower construction in USA and abroad. Married Emma Ruth Dawkins, Coffeeville, Mississippi, who accompanied me on most of my travels. Spent several years in Belize, Central America building towers for government and diving for oil field seismograph pads. Currently farm old home place in Yalobusha County and write semi-fiction tales about many unusual co-workers and our humorous mis-adventures. Have one son and two grandchildren residing in Oxford, Mississippi.

Riding up to work

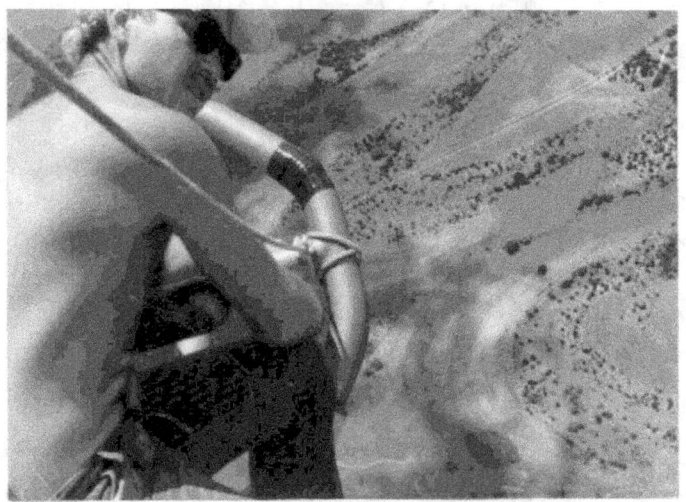
Jon Hovey working on TV Antenna

WLBT 2063' TV Tower

Painted new I-10 Bridge over Mississippi River at Baton Rouge

Hovey House Belize, Central America Jungle

Mahogany Dory/Boat Belize Central America

'TARAWA' CVA-10

www.ingramcontent.com/pod-product-compliance
Lightning Source LLC
Chambersburg PA
CBHW070106120526
44588CB00032B/1158